LIGHT of the DHARMA

LIGHT of the DHARMA

Hoshu Y. Matsubayashi

Edited by
Shobo Gary Jaskula,
Kaigo Matthew Wise,
Joko Cheryl Ikemiya,
Hakushu Hugh Matsubayashi

AMERICAN BUDDHIST STUDY CENTER PRESS
NEW YORK

LIGHT of the DHARMA

Published by American Buddhist Study Center Press,
New York, NY

Printed on 10% recycled paper with soy inks
Printed in the United States of America

Library of Congress Cataloging-in-Publication Data
Hoshu Y. Matsubayashi,
Light of the Dharma
ISBN 978-0-9911360-0-1

CONTENTS

FOREWORD

I am much honored to write this foreword to Rev. Dr. Hoshu Y. Matsubayashi's publication Light of the Dharma.

The word sutra in Sanskrit means warp—a series of threads running lengthwise across a loom. The warp is crossed by another series of threads called the weft.

This book has been beautifully woven because it has good warp of the Buddha-dharma throughout. I see this book as Rev. Matsubayashi's life tapestry, interwoven with the weft of his many life experiences in Japan, the Hongwanji Mission of Hawaii, the Buddhist Churches of America, and the Jodo Shinshu Buddhist Temples of Canada where he served as minister.

Rev. Matsubayashi was one of my first professors at the Institute of Buddhist Studies when I enrolled in the 1970s. He is a passionate minister who has a deep appreciation of the Buddha-dharma. However, he is not just a minister; he is a scholar who is always challenging himself by raising his academic foundation. Rev. Matsubayashi has been my teacher throughout my ministry in this country, and he encourages me to keep studying. He likes to study but he also likes to mingle with people, and whenever he interacts with others he shares how much he appreciates the Dharma.

The Buddhist Churches of America is very fortunate to have Rev. Dr. Hoshu Y. Matsubayashi as our minister who has remained active during his retirement. I sincerely hope that this book, Light of the Dharma, will shed warm light on your life and help make your weft strong so that you can weave your own life tapestry.

In Gassho,
Rev. Kodo Umezu
Bishop

PREFACE

According to Japanese tradition, the age of 77 is designated as a Year of Joy. I enjoyed a year of joy after my full retirement from the ministry at the end of 2012. As a project of my year of joy, I am pleased to publish my new book, Light of the Dharma, from the American Buddhist Study Center Press under the guidance of President Hoshina Seki.

For grateful karmic associations during my ministry, I am happy to include the portraits of Gold Medalist Kristi Yamaguchi and Astronaut Ellison Onizuka in my book. I wish to thank Kristi Yamaguchi, NASA, and Lorna Onizuka for their permission to print the portraits in my book. I am very proud of Kristi and Ellison for their fulfillment (siddha) of their goals (artha) like Siddhartha Gautama.

I wish to thank the Minister's Assistants of the New York Buddhist Church, Shobo Gary Jaskula, Kaigo Matthew Wise, Joko Cheryl Ikemiya, and my son, Hakushu Hugh Matsubayashi, who contributed and assisted in the compilation of this publication.

I wish also to thank Bishop Kodo Umezu of the Buddhist Churches of America for writing the Forward to this book. Last but not least, I appreciate my wife, Kyoko, for her assistance and constant encouragement of my studies in Buddha Dharma.

Hoshu Y. Matsubayashi
Fremont, California
Spring 2014

Chapter I- INTRODUCTION

Light of the Dharma, 50 Years

-Religion of the people, by the people, for the people-

Under the guiding light of the Dharma, I became a minister (*Kaikyoshi*) of the Honpa Hongwanji Mission of Hawaii on September 1, 1959. Over the last 50 years, I have served as a minister of the Honpa Hongwanji Mission of Hawaii, the Buddhist Churches of America, the Buddhist Churches of Canada, and then again for the Buddhist Churches of America, until my retirement on July 31, 2010. After my official retirement, I also served as the full-time resident minister of the New York Buddhist Church from October 1, 2010 to December 31, 2012.

The propagation of Jodo Shinshu Buddhism on the mainland of the United States officially began with the arrival of Hongwanji-dispatched ministers, Rev. Dr. Shue Sonoda and Rev. Kakuryo Nishijima, in San Francisco on September 1, 1899. Thus, the Buddhist Churches of America has existed for over 114 years on the mainland of the United States. I am grateful for having lived under the guiding light of the Buddha Dharma and for the dedicated ministers and followers who have worked so diligently to maintain and develop the teachings of Jodo Shinshu Buddhism in the United States of America.

Rev. Emyo Imamura, who laid the foundation for the Honpa Hongwanji Mission of Hawaii and served as its Bishop for over 32 years, stated the following in his collection of Dharma talks, entitled "Shinran's Teaching and the Characteristics of the United States."

The first characteristic of the United States is democracy; and the second is individualism... Then, what is the characteristic of Shinran's teaching? Needless to say, Shinshu is the most democratic denomination among all of the Buddhist schools. There is a famous expression by President Abraham Lincoln, "Government of the people, by the people, for the people." Shinshu is also a "Religion of the people, by the people, for the people." And it is a religion of individualism, in a certain way. Individualism means that the individual has the ability to seek and develop personal happiness. Shinshu teaches that its main purpose is to seek an individual awakening and joyfulness. Shinran once expressed, "When I carefully reflect upon the Vow which Amida Buddha brought forth after five kalpas of contemplation, I find that it was only for me, Shinran, alone!"

Such individual awakening is individualism in its broadest and most profound meaning, according to Bishop Imamura. Therefore, Jodo Shinshu is never in conflict with democracy or individualism. Bishop Imamura often reminded Nembutsu followers, who immigrated to the United States from Japan, that Jodo Shinshu is a wonderful religion to follow in this country.

Miyoko Kaneta, a retired schoolteacher in Seattle, who was raised in central California, recorded "A Song of Praise for *Issei* Pioneers." She translated the lyrics of that song into English as follows:

Far distant in a land vast and wild,
Bravely toiling the great Rocky Mountains,
In this land of great abundance and wealth,
Issei pioneers seeking their livelihood, their fortune,
Ah–, memories of our fathers.

From the wrinkles on her forehead,
To the palms of her hands,
Holding me in her left arm,

A hoe in her right hand,
Ah–, the unforgettable figure of our mothers.

We live this day, grateful to our parents,
Deep emotions now move me to tears,
For we would not be here but for them,
And today, we stand firmly,
Here, on this land.

Over the course of my 50 years as a minister, I have learned about and witnessed the dedicated efforts of the Issei pioneers and the Nembutsu followers. Jodo Shinshu Buddhism teaches us to listen to the Buddha Dharma in order to awaken to the Infinite Light of Amida Buddha. In his writings, Rennyo Shonin instructed us in how to listen to the Buddha Dharma. These are the words of Rennyo Shonin: "Even though we do not have spare time, we should listen to the Buddha Dharma. It is wrong to think that we should listen to the Buddha Dharma only when we have spare time. The Buddha Dharma teaches us that we never know for sure if we have tomorrow."

Rennyo Shonin encouraged us to listen to the Buddha Dharma with special determination in order to be awakened to the Compassionate Heart of Amida Buddha.

When I was a resident minister at the Southern Alameda County Buddhist Church, a certain member of the Church went back to Japan to see his 84-year-old mother in the hospital. When he met her in the hospital, she asked her son, who was a very busy businessman running multiple companies, "Are you attending church?" He answered, "I am very busy, so I cannot attend church as I wish to." His mother said, "Please attend church first. Then you can say, 'I am busy.'"

When I heard this, I immediately recalled Rennyo Shonin's words, "Listen to the Buddha Dharma, even though you do not have spare time." Her wonderful message was essentially the same as Rennyo Shonin's. The word "busy" in Japanese is often equated with a loss of heart. If we fail to see the heart of the Buddha, the heart of our mother, and the hearts of people, we are not able to awaken to the truth of our lives.

Under the guiding light of the Dharma for over 50 years, I have been able to carry on my ministry with the support and friendship of countless Dharma friends in the Honpa Hongwanji Mission of Hawaii, the Buddhist Churches of Canada (presently the Jodo Shinshu Buddhist Temples of Canada), and the Buddhist Churches of America. How grateful I am for over 50 years of a minister's life.

BCA Wheel of Dharma, July 2010 (Revised)

The Three Treasures: Buddha, Dharma, and Sangha

-Wisdom (*Prajna*) and Compassion (*Karuna*)-

The Preamble of the By-Laws of the Buddhist Churches of America states that "each member shall honor the Three Treasures: Buddha, Dharma, and Sangha; and follow faithfully the teaching of Shinran Shonin according to Jodo Shinshu Hongwanji-ha." Thus, having a heart which honors the Three Treasures of Buddha, Dharma, and Sangha is the fundamental characteristic of all ministers and laypeople in the Buddhist Churches of America.

Prince Shotoku (574-624 C.E.), who is considered to be the founder of Japanese Buddhism, and who, even today, is highly respected by the Japanese people, set down the first *Seventeen Article Constitution* in Japan in order to govern the country during the early seventh century. The Second Article of the Constitution, like the Preamble of the By-Laws of BCA, declares that the people will "Sincerely honor the Three Treasures. The Three Treasures are Buddha, Dharma, and Sangha …"

The word *Buddha* means an enlightened one who has the Wisdom (*prajna*) to see the truth of the world. Buddha also means wisdom itself, which works through compassion (*karuna*). The Wisdom and Compassion of the Buddha is the guiding light for all people of the Buddhist Churches of America.

Dharma is the teachings of Buddha. It also means the laws and principles of things in the universe. Shakyamuni Buddha once said about Dharma that "Although I expound the Dharma, Dharma has existed eternally regardless of my birth or not." Shakyamuni Buddha moved Dharma into action for the first time in our human history. And the history of the Buddhist Churches of America has been and will be guided by the eternal Dharma.

Sangha means a harmonious gathering of Buddhists who are

living with the Buddha of Infinite Light (Wisdom) and Infinite Life (Compassion).

My late uncle, who was a movie director at the Toho Movie Company in Japan, once described the importance of lights in his movie studio such that "even when all the studio lights are turned off, the single faint light on the ceiling of the stage remains on. That light shows us the way out. We refer to that ceiling light as the eternal nightlight (*Joya-to*). That eternal nightlight remains on even when the studio lights that consume hundreds of kilowatts of power are on. During my 30 years as a movie director, I have always been moved by this eternal nightlight that remains on after all the studio lights are turned off. We were always able to exit safely from the dark studio guided by that eternal nightlight."

Although the Buddha's light of Wisdom and Compassion is constantly shining upon us, we often fail to realize such Buddha light.

The eternal nightlight (*Joya-to*) on the ceiling of the studio stage is like the compassionate light that is constantly shining on everyone, but which people fail to appreciate because of their passions.

Shinran Shonin declared that we must take refuge in the Buddha of Infinite Life (Compassion) and Light (Wisdom) in the beginning of the Shoshin-ge. "I take refuge in the Buddha of Infinite Life" (*Kimyo Muryo-jyu Nyorai*) and "I take refuge in the Buddha of Inconceivable Light" (*Namo Fukashigi-ko*). Jodo Shinshu Buddhism begins by taking refuge in the Buddha of Compassion and Wisdom. This is the essential guidance of the Buddhist Churches of America.

The Essentials of Jodo Shinshu Buddhism

Jodo Shinshu Buddhism, which is a branch of Mahayana Buddhism, was founded by Shinran (1173-1262 C.E.) and is one of the largest Buddhist denominations in Japan today. The doctrine of Jodo Shinshu Buddhism depends upon the Three Pure Land Sutras. These sutras expound upon Amida Buddha and his land, and the method for attaining Buddhahood. The sutras are:

1. *Larger Sukhavativyuha Sutra*
2. *Amitayurdhyana Sutra*
3. *Smaller Sukhavativyuha Sutra*

Shinran interpreted the Three Pure Land Sutras in two ways. First, he considered the *Larger Sukhavativyuha Sutra* to be the true teaching of Shakyamuni Buddha and stated in his main writing, *Kyogyoshinsho* (*Teaching, Practice, Awakening, and Enlightenment*), that "to reveal the true teaching: it is the *Larger Sukhavativyuha Sutra of Infinite Life...*" It teaches the Buddha's Primal (18th) Vow; and this is the intent of the Sutra. Second, Shinran taught that all three of the Pure Land sutras expound on the true essence of Shakyamuni Buddha's teachings. The *Larger Sukhavativyuha Sutra* teaches the truth of the Dharma; the *Amitayurdhyana Sutra* teaches the truth of human nature and contemplation on the Buddha; and the *Smaller Sukhavativyuha Sutra* describes the Dharma, human nature, and the praises of Amida Buddha by various Buddhas. Therefore, Shinran believed that all three of the Pure Land sutras teach the truth of Shakyamuni Buddha.

After Jodo Shinshu Buddhism was introduced to Hawaii in 1889 and to the mainland of the United States in 1899, it spread all over the world as a global religion.

The main teaching of Jodo Shinshu Buddhism is the Universal Vow of Compassion and Wisdom of Amida Buddha, who has Infinite Life and Infinite Light. Since Infinite Life means "always" and Infinite Light means "everywhere," Jodo Shinshu Buddhism is a religion for all people in any place and at any time. Shinran reminded us that Amida Buddha is constantly shining upon everyone with his guiding light of Great Compassion and Wisdom. And the recitation of the Nembutsu, "Namo Amida Butsu," in Jodo Shinshu Buddhism is the realization of oneness with that Great Compassion and Wisdom of Amida Buddha.

Because Shinran was teaching the Nembutsu to the ordinary people of Japan, with his Master Honen, he was exiled into the northern country by the Japanese government. But, after he was pardoned, he continued to propagate the Nembutsu in order that these ordinary people could attain enlightenment in these remote areas. He taught that the Universal Vow of Amida Buddha does not discriminate against anyone because of their social status, physical conditions, or lifestyle. Shinran expressed joyfully in the *Tanni-sho* (*Notes Lamenting Differences*) the following:

"When I carefully consider the Universal Vow, which Amida Buddha brought forth, I find that it was only for me, Shinran, alone! How gracious is the Universal Vow of Amida Buddha who resolved to lead me to enlightenment!"

After Shinran passed away and as time went on, Shinran's real teachings were truly recognized in Japan; and Jodo Shinshu Buddhism became one of the largest denominations. In 1877, six hundred and fourteen years after his death, the Emperor Meiji of Japan honored Shinran with the special title of "Kenshin Daishi," which means "The Great Teacher Who Revealed the Truth." Jodo Shinshu Buddhism, as the global religion of the Universal Vow of Amida Buddha, will be able to contribute to world peace and civilization.

What is the Nembutsu, Namo Amida Butsu?

The Nembutsu is the fundamental teaching of Jodo Shinshu Buddhism; and Shinran taught the true and real meaning of the Nembutsu. The summary of Jodo Shinshu Buddhist teachings is expressed in two phrases: "Shinjin Sho-in (Entrusting heart is the true cause of birth into the Pure Land)" and "Shomyo Hoon (The recitation of the Nembutsu is one's gratitude to Amida Buddha)."

It is very important for the followers of Jodo Shinshu Buddhism to understand the true and real meaning of the Nembutsu as expounded by Shinran, and to carry on the Nembutsu in their lives.

The original meaning of the Nembutsu is "Thought of Buddha" (*Buddha-smriti*). In the history of Buddhism, the Nembutsu has been practiced in various ways. And following many years of doctrinal developments by the Seven Masters, Shinran finally established the true Nembutsu teaching of Jodo Shinshu Buddhism.

The Nembutsu, *Namo Amida Butsu*, is a Japanese transliteration of the Sanskrit phrases *Namas Amitabha* (Infinite Light) and *Namas Amitayus* (Infinite Life). When a Sanskrit word that ends with "-as" is followed by a word which begins with a vowel, the "-as" changes to an "-o." Therefore, we spell the Nembutsu as *Namo Amida Butsu* or *Namu Amida Butsu*.

In the book, *The Way of Nirvana*, Dr. Ryosetsu Fujiwara, former professor of the Institute of Buddhist Studies in Berkeley, describes such various forms of the Nembutsu as follows: "... in the history of Buddhist practices there appeared many special forms of the Nembutsu. The Goe Nembutsu (Fivefold Rhythmical Nembutsu Recitation), for example, was introduced to Japan by Ennin (794-864 C.E.) of the Tendai School from China. This Nembutsu later developed into the Fudan Nembutsu (Incessant Recitation of the Nembutsu) and the Inzei Nembutsu (Chanting of the Nembutsu with a

Prolonged Voice). As ritual practices of the Nembutsu, there appeared the Yuzu Nembutsu (Nembutsu of Inter-Penetrating in All Beings), the Kan Nembutsu (One Month Practice during Winter Nights, Striking Gongs and Chanting Nembutsu), the Uta Nembutsu (Chanting of Nembutsu in Tones), and the Odori Nembutsu (Chanting of Nembutsu Combined with the Striking of Gongs and Drums, Singing of Psalms, and Dancing). The last one was initiated by Kuya (903-972 C.E.) and made more popular by Ippen (1239-1289 C.E.)."

Since there are various kinds of Nembutsu, it is important to understand the true and real meaning of the Nembutsu in Jodo Shinshu Buddhism. One important question about this Nembutsu is whether it is a type of prayer or not.

In the early twentieth century, the drama *Shukke to Sono Deshi* (*The Priest and His Disciples*), written by Hyakuzo Kurata (1891-1943), was a best seller. It describes the love and passion between Yuien, a disciple of Shinran, and Kaede, a prostitute. Both try to live truly and sincerely to their human natures and seek guidance from Shinran.

Glenn W. Shaw translated the drama into English in 1922, translating the Nembutsu, "Namu Amida Butsu," as "Save us, oh, Amida Buddha!" One Shinshu Buddhist objected to this rendering of the Nembutsu, since it is not a prayer. However, Shaw did not change the rendering of the Nembutsu in his 1955 edition and stated in his preface the following:

> *"He (a Shinshu Buddhist) wanted a positive and affirmative rendering, something like 'Hail, oh, Amida Buddha!' or 'Amida Buddha, Amen!' He was right enough for himself and many like him, but for a frightened old lady whose house is burning down, for instance, the commonly used, less philosophical sense would doubtless be more nearly correct."*

In other words, Shaw insisted that the recitation of the Nembutsu under adverse circumstances could not be considered an expression of gratitude or positive.

However, Amida Buddha is constantly extending his Wisdom and Compassion to everyone who is living in countless Karmic conditions. To be awakened to the function (Primal Vow) of Amida Buddha, who has such Great Wisdom and Compassion, means to live with the Nembutsu, Namo Amida Butsu. As a result of awakening to the Primal Vow of Amida Buddha, the Nembutsu, "Namo Amida Butsu," becomes the energy and power by which to live. Shinran reminded us of this in the *Tanni-sho* (*Notes Lamenting Differences*), that "The Nembutsu is the Unimpeded Single Path."

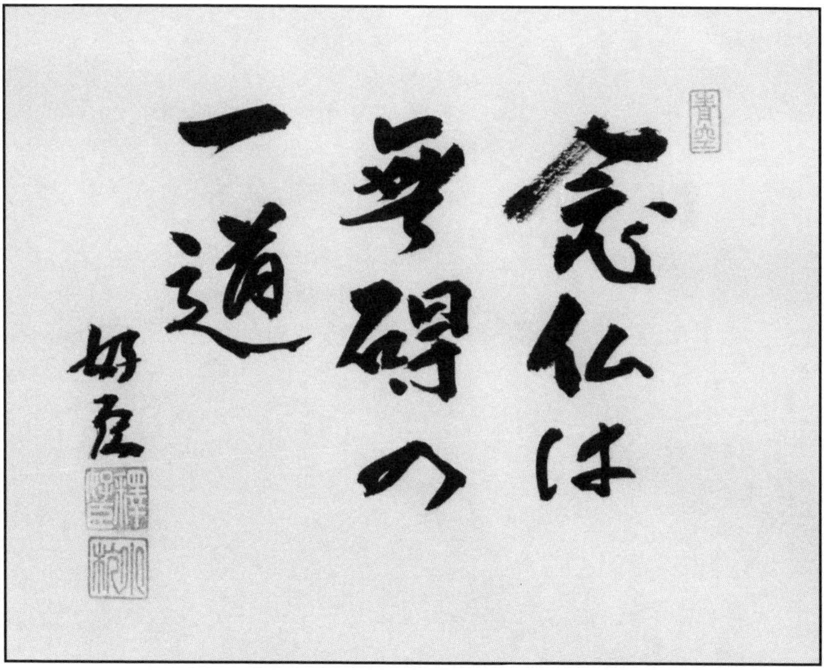

The Unimpeded Single Path

Chapter II-
TEACHINGS OF THE BUDDHA IN SOCIETY

Nivana in Football

We find a few Buddhist Sanskrit terms in English dictionaries nowadays. One of the most popular Buddhist Sanskrit words is "Nirvana." *Webster's New World Dictionary* gives two definitions of the word "Nirvana," according to Hinduism and Buddhism. Newspaper reporters and other writers often use Buddhist Sanskrit terms to describe complicated situations with a single word.

When my two sons were attending the University of California in Berkeley in 1990, there was a big cross-bay football game between Berkeley and Stanford. It was their 93rd meeting and Berkeley's Memorial Stadium was packed with more than 75,000 spectators, including students from both universities.

These games often became wild with excitement. One such exciting game was in 1982. Stanford was winning the game up until the final seconds. However, some Stanford marching band members came out onto the field before the game was actually over; and a Berkeley player rushed with the ball through the Stanford band members and made a touchdown, thus reversing the game in the last few seconds for a dramatic Berkeley win. It was kind of comical scene, which later appeared on T-shirts with the word "Play."

Another almost unbelievable thing happened again in the big game of 1990. Berkeley was leading Stanford, 25-18, with 12 seconds to go. Berkeley made a touchdown; and some of the Berkeley fans came out onto the field before the game was actually over. For this, Berkeley was penalized 9 points in the last 12 seconds, losing the game with a score of 27-25. This 93rd game was called the "biggest of the big games."

The following day, a sportswriter for The San Francisco Examiner, Spender Art, wrote, "a touchdown in the football game was Nirvana." I was impressed by his usage of this Sanskrit word, "Nirvana." The Nirvana of the touchdown, which decided the big game in the last seconds, was the final and ultimate goal, which will last forever as a winner.

When Siddhartha Gautama attained enlightenment at the age of 35, his enlightenment was the final goal of Nirvana; while at the same time, Nirvana began his activities as the Buddha.

Therefore, we can appreciate the Compassion and Wisdom of Amida Buddha anytime and anywhere. Death in Buddhism means birth into the Pure Land of the Buddha. It is a beginning of the activities of the Buddha.

"Things Invisible Are Still There"

There was a beautiful woman poet named Misuzu Kaneko in Nagato City, Yamaguchi Prefecture, in Japan. She was born in 1903 and wrote many poems that took a gentle and profound look at all things earthly, as well as cosmic.

In 2003, the 100th anniversary of the birth of the poet, Misuzu, was celebrated in her hometown. One of her poems, entitled "Stars and a Dandelion," from her book, *Matsuge no Niji* (*Rainbows on Eyelashes*), stated:

In the deep blue sky,
Like the pebbles at the bottom of the sea,
The daytime stars, sinking until night comes,
Are invisible to our eyes.
But though we can't see them, they are there.
Things invisible are still there.

June is the month of commencement ceremonies. Many students graduate in June. To graduate is a big step. Some of the graduates will go on to higher their education. Others will find jobs, while others will go on to travel.

No matter what the step or how large, Amida Buddha will always be there. The Buddha cannot make any decision for these people; but the Buddha will guide them in every way. Everyone must challenge the world oneself.

Buddhism reminds us of the "Four Kinds of Indebtedness" (*On* in Japanese), which everyone receives in everyday life. The Japanese word *On* is difficult to translate into English. It means indebtedness, kindness, goodness, a favor, and a debt of gratitude. People receive care and love from their parents, guidance from their teachers, support from numerous living beings, and guidance from the Buddha. Most of this guidance, care, kindness, and love, which leads to debts of gratitude, is invisible. Yet many of the Japanese immigrant parents dedicated their lives to it for the sake of their children.

Just as the Japanese poet Misuzu Kaneko reminds us in her poem, "Things invisible are still there." Spiritual eyes should be opened to see things that are invisible and be awakened to a life of gratitude.

Shinran reminded us also to rejoice. For, although we fail to appreciate it, Amida Buddha's great compassionate light is always cast upon us, which he described in his Hymns of the Pure Land Masters in the following poem:

> *Although my eyes, blinded by passions,*
> *Do not see the Amida Buddha's light which embraces me.*
> *The Great Compassion never tires,*
> *Always casting compassionate light upon me.*

Amida Buddha's compassionate light is always guiding us in everyday life.

Shinran's Tears of Joy and Sorrow

-To Attain the State of Enlightenment-

In the early morning of Sunday, September 7, 2008, an NHK educational program, *The Spiritual Era – Religion and Human Life*, was broadcast on television. The speaker was lecturer Wei Zhang of Dobo University; and her topic was "Led by Shinran's Tears."

Ms. Zhang was born in Changchu, China, and experienced the Chinese Cultural Revolution. She experienced fierce incidents during the Revolution, and started to work on a translation of the writings of a Japanese proletarian novelist, Hiroshi Noma. While she was working on the Chinese translations of Noma's writings, she learned about Shinran Shonin. For Mr. Noma presented her with Shinran's main writing, *Kyogyoshinsho*, (*Teaching, Practice, Awakening, and Enlightenment*) and other of his writings. After she studied Shinran's works, she wrote a book, entitled *Literature of Hiroshi Noma and Shinran – Logic of Salvation for Evils*; and she also published a book of her public lectures, entitled *The Nembutsu Echoes Beyond the Ocean.*

The tears mentioned in her speech, "Led by Shinran's Tears," can be explained in an excerpt from the *Tanni-sho* (*Notes Lamenting Differences*), Chapter II. "Since I am incapable of any practice whatsoever, hell would definitely be my dwelling anyway." Shinran cried tears of sorrow when he had the profound realization of his own human nature, which disabled him from attaining enlightenment. This realization is the same as Shantao's realization that "I have no chance for liberation." In his tears of sorrow, he found that the absolute compassion of Amida Buddha, which embraces all people, leads to enlightenment. Ms. Zhang discovered the essence of Shinran's teachings, the assurance that ordinary people will attain enlightenment through Amida Buddha's compassion.

She found the essence of Shinran's teachings in the *Shoshin-ge* (*Hymn of True Faith on the Nembutsu*) in the following lines:

> *When ordinary people and sages, as well as those who commit the gravest offenses and abusers of the Buddha Dharma are taken into the Amida Buddha's Primal Vow, they become one in spiritual attainment, just as many rivers become of one taste upon entering the sea.*

As Ms. Zhang pointed out, when Shinran was awakened to the absolute compassion of Amida Buddha, his tears of sorrow turned into tears of joy.

> *The essence of Shinran's teachings reminds us that, in order to turn tears of sorrow into tears of joy, one has to be awakened to Amida Buddha's Wisdom and Compassion. The Shoshin-ge (Hymn of True Faith on the Nembutsu) explains that ordinary people can attain enlightenment with their human natures as follows: If the single thought of entrusting heart in Amida Buddha is awakened in us, we shall attain Nirvana without severing our blind passions.*

Shinran encouraged us to entrust in Amida Buddha's Primal Vow in order to attain enlightenment by stating the following in the Hymns of the Dharma-Ages:

> *Entrust yourself to Amida Buddha's Primal Vow.*
> *Through the benefit of being grasped, never to be abandoned,*
> *All who entrust themselves to the Primal Vow*
> *Attain the supreme enlightenment.*

Thus, Shinran Shonin taught that all people could attain enlightenment without severing one's own blind passions (*Klesa* in Sanskrit; *Bonno* in Japanese), if we are awakened to Amida Buddha's Primal Vow.

KISB: The Poetry of Shinran Shonin

-Shinran's Equation Theory-

One of the most unforgettable speeches that I have heard in my life was the keynote address at my son's college graduation ceremony. My oldest son graduated from the College of Engineering of the University of California at Berkeley on May 23, 1987. The ceremony was held at the Hearst Greek Theatre with over 10,000 people in attendance, including professors, graduates, and guests. It was one day before the 50th anniversary of the opening of the Golden Gate Bridge in May 1937.

The keynote speaker was Professor John R. Whinnery of the Department of Electrical Engineering and Computer Sciences. Prof. Whinnery graduated from U.C. Berkeley in 1937 with a B.S. in Electrical Engineering. He was awarded the campus' highest scholastic honor, the University Medal. He became a microwave and laser expert, and received the National Medal of Science in June 1992.

The title of his speech was "KISG (Keep It Simple, Graduates!): The Poetry of Einstein, Maxwell, and Joseph Strauss." He explained that "The Poetry" is like a Japanese Haiku poem, the simplest poem. He was encouraging the graduates to use the vast knowledge that they had acquired at the University to achieve simple designs and to avoid unnecessary complexity.

Albert Einstein was one of the greatest scientists of the 20th century, having discovered the Mass Energy Equation. James Maxwell discovered the basic equations of electromagnetism. And Joseph Strauss was the Chief Engineer of the famous Golden Gate Bridge in San Francisco, a bridge that many thought would be impossible to build. Their achievements were the result of simplicity out of vast knowledge.

After I heard Prof. Whinnery's speech, I came up with my own simpler understanding of Shinran Shonin's teaching of Jodo Shinshu Buddhism. It is said that Shakyamuni Buddha taught

84,000 different teachings according to the needs of the people who wanted to attain enlightenment. Shinran Shonin discovered a unique equation theory after he studied numerous teachings of Shakyamuni Buddha and the Seven Masters of India, China, and Japan. He taught that the Nembutsu, Namo Amida Butsu, is the true and simplest way to attain enlightenment.

"KISB (Keep It Simple, Buddhists!): The Poetry of Shinran Shonin." Shinran's Equation Theory is "Namo (I) = Amida Butsu, I am equal with Amida Buddha." We become one with the Infinite Life and Light of the Buddha when we are awakened to the Primal Vow of Amida Buddha.

Shinran Shonin is the great teacher, who discovered the Equation Theory of the Nembutsu, Namo Amida Butsu, which assures everyone that they will become the Buddha, the Enlightened One.

Chapter III- TEACHINGS OF THE BUDDHA IN THE ANNUAL BUDDHIST OBSERVANCES

A Beautiful and Happy New Year

On July 4, 2006, the winning essay in an "America the Beautiful" essay contest, written by 13-year-old Allison Crha, was published in *The Seattle Times*. Her essay was very impressive. She stated, "America's majestic landscapes and breath-taking views are indeed beautiful; but America's true beauty lies in the hearts of her people." She also wrote, "Americans have the opportunity to learn about different cultures and religions. This diversity found in America makes our country stronger."

Since my wife and I came to New York in October 2010, we have been experiencing and observing the beauty of America in this greatest city in the world! When my wife was stuck at the turnstile of the subway, after she swiped her senior citizen's MetroCard and it did not work, a lady, who had just come out from subway, swiped her MetroCard (not a senior citizen's card) and let my wife go in. And then she just walked away. My wife did not have a chance to thank her. We also enjoyed the wonderful people of different religious and cultural backgrounds who attended the services.

I was born at the Olaa (currently Puna) Hongwanji Mission in Hawaii before World War II. The temple was located in the middle of a sugar cane field on the way to Volcano from Hilo. Life in those days was not easy because it was in the early stages of the Japanese immigration to Hawaii, and at a time of the economic recession in the 1930s. Despite such hardship and discrimination, the Japanese Issei immigrant parents brought up their Nisei children with the determination of "For the Sake of Children" (*Kodomo no Tameni*). Their children, young Niseis, joined the U.S. Army to fight for our country during World War II; and many of them made the ultimate sacrifice. They all contributed to making our country stronger. I wonder if Allison Crha was thinking about the sacrifices of those immigrant children when she was writing her winning essay.

Rennyo Shonin was severe with his disciples and followers in urging them to follow the way of the Nembutsu life. Such admonitions are expressed in the *Record of Rennyo Shonin's Words*. In Article 1 of the book, Rennyo Shonin advised one of his followers, named Dotoku, who came to see Rennyo Shonin on New Year's Day, and asked him, "How old are you, Dotoku? Recite the Nembutsu." Also, in Article 17, Rennyo Shonin admonished his disciple Junsei, who came to express year-end gratitude to Rennyo Shonin, that "For the expression of year-end gratitude, you should be awakened to the true and real faith in Amida Buddha."

Rennyo Shonin also stated in his Epistles (*Gobunsho*), Volume 1, No. 3, that "As long as we live, we should recite the Nembutsu with gratitude. These people are called the followers of true faith, who have established peaceful minds." Rennyo Shonin's reminder of the recitation of the Nembutsu in gratitude on New Year's Day should be the best message of the New Year for Jodo Shinshu Buddhists.

It would be nice if everyone were to live in oneness with the compassionate hearts of their departed parents and Amida Buddha in the Nembutsu, *Namo Amida Butsu*, throughout the year.

"America's true beauty," according to Allison Crha, "lies in the hearts of her people." A life of the Nembutsu truly reflects the beautiful hearts of Jodo Shinshu Buddhists. When people welcome a new year with their beautiful hearts, the year becomes certainly beautiful.

With this feeling of gratitude, Buddhists are able to live their daily lives positively, just as has been stated in the following poem by Ko Hirasawa, M.D., former President of Kyoto University and a Nembutsu follower himself, in his book entitled *Sah, Ganbarou* (*Now, Let's Work Hard!*):

Today is wonderful; tomorrow will be wonderful, and also the day after tomorrow: Every day is wonderful in gratitude, wonderful, wonderful, and wonderful!

Nirvana With A Residue & Nirvana Without A Residue

Shakyamuni Buddha entered into Pari (Great)-Nirvana on February 15th over 2,500 years ago under the Sala tree at Kushinagara in India at the age of 80. This Nirvana is called "Nirvana Without a Residue." Mahayana Buddhists observe the Nirvana Day Service on this day in the month of February.

After Prince Siddhartha renounced his luxurious royal life at the age of 29, he did ascetic practices for six years. Then, giving up these ascetic practices, he meditated under the Bodhi tree and attained the state of Nirvana at the age of 35. He became the Buddha, the Enlightened One. This Nirvana is called "Nirvana With a Residue or his Physical Body." Whoever attains such a state of Nirvana is called the Buddha, the Enlightened One. Then, as the Buddha, Shakyamuni began to propagate the Buddha Dharma for the next forty-five years.

His first Buddha Dharma talk after his enlightenment was at Deer Park and is called the "Wheel of the Dharma in Motion for the First Time." Mahayana Buddhists celebrate this Day of Enlightenment as Bodhi Day on December 8th.

According to the *Monier-Williams' Sanskrit-English Dictionary*, Nirvana means, "blown or put out, extinguished…" Prince Siddhartha was able to extinguish or destroy all his evil passions (*Klesa*) to attain the state of Nirvana.

When Shakyamuni Buddha was near death, after forty-five years of propagation of the Buddha Dharma, he addressed his disciples in his last teaching as follows:

> *It may be that some of you will think, 'The word of The Teacher is a thing of the past; we now have no teacher.' But that is not the correct view. The Dharma, which I have taught and enjoyed upon you, is to be your teacher when I am gone. Make of yourself a light. Rely upon yourself. Make the Dharma your light. Rely upon the Dharma.*

Thus, he advised his followers to "Make of oneself a light" (*Ji-tomyo*) and "Make the Dharma one's light" (*Ho-tomyo*). Then he entered into Pari-Nirvana.

Shinran Shonin, founder of Jodo Shinshu Buddhism, reminded us that both Shakyamuni Buddha and Amida Buddha are trying to lead people to enlightenment. He praised Shakyamuni Buddha and Amida Buddha in his poems, "The Hymns on the Pure Land Masters," as follows:

> *Shakyamuni Buddha and Amida Buddha*
> *Are Compassionate parents:*
> *Using all means they skillfully lead us*
> *And in us the supreme Faith*
> *Do they awaken.*

The Nirvana of Shakyamuni Buddha does not always dwell in quiescence; but it actively works for the benefit of all sentient beings. Nirvana is the ultimate goal for Buddhists; it is the initial function of the Enlightened One, the Buddha. It is stated in Shan-tao's writing, "To understand the Buddha is to awaken to the Great Compassionate Heart." Amida Buddha, as the Compassionate Buddha, is always acting everywhere and anytime for the benefit of all people wishing to attain Nirvana.

On this Nirvana Day, make oneself a guiding light and make the Dharma our guiding light. We will be awakened to the Great Compassion of Amida Buddha by listening to the Dharma as our guiding light, as our teacher.

Spring Ohigan

-The Other Shore of the Buddha's World -

In Buddhism, the practice of the "Six Kinds of Perfection" (*Paramita* in Sanskrit) leads people to reach the other shore (*Ohigan*) of enlightenment, the world of the Buddha. By fulfilling these Six Kinds of Perfection, one can become the Buddha, the Enlightened One. These Six Kinds of Perfection (*Paramita*) are: 1. *Dana* (Giving), 2. *Sila* (Precepts), 3. *Ksanti* (Perseverance), 4. *Virya* (Effort), 5. *Dhyana* (Meditation), and 6. *Prajna* (Wisdom).

Since it is very difficult for ordinary people to fulfill these Six Perfections, Shinran Shonin, the founder of Jodo Shinshu Buddhism, taught a way to attain enlightenment by awakening the wisdom and compassion of Amida Buddha. The world of the Buddha is described in the *Small Pure Land Sutra* as, "From here to the west, beyond ten billion Buddha-lands, there is a world called the Pure Land. In that land, there is Amida Buddha. He is now, at present, preaching the Dharma." This geographical description of the Buddha's world in the scriptures may be difficult for people to understand with a 21st century view of the universe.

Then, how can people understand this description?

Ryunosuke Akutagawa, a famous author in Japan, who wrote the story upon which the movie Rashomon is based, once said that "the difference between a genius and an ordinary person is only a piece of paper, but in order to transcend that piece of paper, people have to make an effort, like walking over one thousand miles." Akutagawa's explanation of a piece of paper and a distance of over one thousand miles may give us an insight into understanding the geographical description of the world of the Buddha. When Saichi Asahara, a devout Jodo Shinshu Buddhist follower, was asked whether it is true or not that the world of the Buddha is beyond ten billion Buddha-lands, as it is described in the scriptures, he replied to his friend "the Buddha is right here with me and the Buddha-land is next to me."

An English- and Japanese-language newspaper in San Francisco once carried an article titled "100 Tanka Poems of Modern Students." Toyo University in Tokyo, Japan, invited Japanese students to enter a Tanka poem contest. Over 63,000 Tanka poems were submitted. One of the 100 selected Tanka poems, composed by a 9th grader, was published as follows:

> *In Japanese,*
> *"Ganbare" to, kuchidewa iwanai, hahanaredo,*
> *Tonkatsu ageru, otode hagemasu.*
>
> *In English,*
> *Though mother does not speak the word, "persevere;"*
> *The sound of frying tonkatsu (a breaded pork cutlet)*
> *encourages me.*

This 9th grader has a wonderful heart of awakening.

An image of this mother, who is cooking for her child, shows her profound loving heart. When the child hears the sound of the frying pork cutlet, it acts as an encouragement to persevere. The child has truly been awakened to the mother's love and compassion, and can hear her thoughts, without hearing her words.

Rennyo Shonin states in his writings, The *Record of Rennyo Shonin's Words*, that "the true prosperity of a temple comes when its members, be it even a single person, obtain enlightenment, then we can say that the temple prospers."

According to Jodo Shinshu Buddhist tradition, the Ohigan service is called a "Gathering for Praising the Buddha" or *San-Butsu-e*. It is a time when Jodo Shinshu Buddhists gather together to praise the Wisdom and Compassion of Amida Buddha and to enjoy happiness in their Nembutsu lives.

Hana Matsuri (Flower Festival)

-The Celebration of Shakyamuni Buddha's Birth-

Hana Matsuri or the Flower Festival is held annually to commemorate the birthday of Shakyamuni Buddha, the founder of Buddhism. On April 8th, in the midst of the sixth century B.C., he was born as prince of the Kapilavastu Castle in India. Shakyamuni's birth took place in the Lumbini Garden, where Queen Maya stopped to rest on her way to her parents' castle. Journeying to the parents' home for the event of giving birth was the custom of the time. According to legend, the baby was born from her right chest as she tried to cut a branch from the Ashoka flowers tree. This indicated that the baby was born into the warrior class. The warrior class was the second highest class of the four-caste system, just below the Brahman or priest class. Those of the Brahma or priest class were believed to be born from the head of the mother.

It is said that the newly born baby took seven steps, pointed his right hand to the sky and his left hand to the earth, and proclaimed, "Above the heaven and below the heaven, I am the Most Honored One." The seven steps indicate the world of enlightenment, which exists beyond the six realms of the unenlightened world. The baby was named Siddhartha, which means "every wish fulfilled."

The legendary story states that sweet rain fell from the sky to bathe the body of the baby. For the Hana Matsuri service, a little shrine is decorated with various beautiful flowers, depicting the beautiful flower garden of Lumbini, where the baby Buddha was born. Inside the flower shrine, a little statue of the baby Buddha is placed in a bowl of "sweet tea." During the service, sweet tea is ladled over the top of statue to bathe the baby Buddha and to celebrate his birth.

Siddhartha lived the royal life as a prince, but this luxurious life did not provide him with true happiness. Having lost his

mother just eight days after his birth, he realized that it was not possible for him to escape completely from the cycle of birth, old age, sickness, and death. He renounced his royal life at the age of 29 to seek the truth of human life. Initially he became a hermit, practicing asceticism. But the physical disciplines did not lead him to true peace. Finally, abandoning both luxurious and ascetic lives, he meditated under the Bodhi tree and became the Enlightened One when he was 35 years old.

Shakyamuni Buddha taught the Four Noble Truths, in order to show us the roots of our sufferings, and taught us the way to attain the state of Nirvana/Enlightenment by presenting the Eightfold Path. These "folds" are Right Understanding, Right Thought, Right Speech, Right Action, Right Livelihood, Right Effort, Right Mindfulness, and Right Meditation.

As he became the great spiritual teacher of the world, he was addressed by numerous honorary titles. Some of these are the Buddha, the Enlightened One; Shakyamuni (*Shakuson*), sage of the Shakya Clan, Tathagata (*Nyorai*), one who has gone to the world of truth (*Thusness*), Arhat (*Arakan*), one who deserves respect; and Bhagavat (*Seson*), one who is honored by the people of the world.

Symbolically speaking, Shakyamuni Buddha expounded 84,000 different teachings for the benefit of all beings. He taught various teachings, just as a physician prescribes medicine according to the diagnosis of the patient. He expounded the teachings in the best way suited to his Sangha so that everyone understood them. Shakyamuni Buddha provided a spiritual medicine or teaching for persons with 84,000 different ills and personalities, in order to lead these diverse people to awaken to enlightenment.

Shinran Shonin appreciated Shakyamuni Buddha's birth in *The Hymns on the Pure Land as follows:*

> *Amida Buddha existing from the eternal past,*
> *Having compassion on the ordinary people*
> *In the world of the five defilements,*

Appeared in the Castle of Kapilavastu
Manifesting himself as Shakyamuni Buddha.

According to Shinran Shonin, the birth of Shakyamuni Buddha as Prince Siddhartha of Kapilavastu Castle was a manifestation of Amida Buddha, who has been extending his compassion from the eternal past.

Although Shakyamuni Buddha taught many different teachings, the sole essence of his teachings is compassion. The *Amitayurdhyana Sutra* states "The Mind of the Buddha is Great Compassion."

Shinran Shonin also appreciated that Shakyamuni Buddha and Amida Buddha are extending great compassion and wisdom to everyone, thus leading to Enlightenment, as stated in *The Hymns of the Dharma-Ages* as follows:

Through the compassion of Shakyamuni and Amida Buddha,
We have been brought to realize the mind that seeks to
attain Nirvana.
By entering into wisdom of a true awakening faith,
We become those who respond
In gratitude to the Buddha's guidance.

The realization of compassion in our lives leads us to a life of awakening. Thus, Buddhism has been in existence of over 2,500 years, guiding the welfare of all beings. The great compassion that Buddhism teaches is essential to a global religion, one that the entire world needs to follow today.

Dr. Edward Conze, a well-known Buddhist scholar, states in his book, *Buddhism: Its Essence and Development*, "The Buddhist community is the oldest institution of mankind. It has survived longer than any other institution except [for] the kindred sect of Jains."

The birthday of the great religious leader, Shakyamuni Buddha, is celebrated as Hana Matsuri or the Flower Festival.

Shinran Shonin ABC Cards

-A Game Similar to Japanese Iroha Karuta-

A. Amida Buddha and Shakyamuni Buddha are our compassionate parents, according to Shinran Shonin.

B. Buddhism was founded by Siddhartha Gautama more than 2,500 years ago.

C. Chinese Masters of Jodo Shinshu Buddhism are T'an-lun (*Donran*, 476 - 542), Tao-ch'o (*Doshaku*, 562 -645), and Shan-tao (*Zendo*, 613 - 681).

D. Dharmakara is the Bodhisattva who became Amida Buddha by fulfilling the 48 Vows.

E. Eshinni-ko is the wife of Shinran Shonin who supported Shinran's propagation of the Nembutsu.

F. Four Noble Truths are the basic teachings of Shakyamuni Buddha, which show the causes and effects of human life and the ultimate goal of Nirvana.

G. Gotan-e commemorates the birthday of Shinran Shonin, the founder of Jodo Shinshu Buddhism.

H. Honen Shonin was the teacher of Shinran Shonin, from whom Shinran learned the teaching of the Nembutsu.

I. Indian Masters of Jodo Shinshu Buddhism are Nagarjuna (*Ryuju, ca.* 150 -250) and Vasubandhu (*Tenjin/Seshin, ca.* 320 - 400).

J. Japanese Masters of Jodo Shinshu Buddhism are Genshin (942 -1017) and Genku (*Honen*, 1133 - 1212).

K. *Kyogyoshinsho or Teaching, Practice, Awakening, and Enlightenment* is the main writing of Shinran Shonin, and it describes the fundamental doctrine of Jodo Shinshu Buddhism.

L. Light and Life of Amida Buddha are Infinite; these are the two major functions of the Wisdom and Compassion of Amida Buddha.

M. Matsuwaka-maro is the childhood name of Shinran Shonin.

N. *Namo Amida Butsu* means, "I am one with the Infinite Light (Wisdom) and the Infinite Life (Compassion) of Amida Buddha.

O. *Oshoko* uses incense to purify our minds in front of Amida Buddha.

P. *Paramita* means "perfection." Six Kinds of Paramitas lead us to the other shore of enlightenment, the world of the Buddha.

Q. Queen Maya is the mother of Prince Siddhartha Gautama.

R. Rennyo Shonin is the Eighth Abbot of Jodo Shinshu Hongwanji–ha, who wrote the *Gobunsho* or Epistles, and explained the essential teachings of Shinran Shonin.

S. Shinran Shonin is the founder of Jodo Shinshu Buddhism, born in Hino village near Kyoto, Japan, on May 21, 1173. We celebrate his birthday as Gotan-e.

T. Triple Sutras of Jodo Shinshu Buddhism are the *Larger Pure Land Sutra*, the *Contemplation on the Buddha of Infinite Life Sutra*, and the *Smaller Pure Land Sutra*.

U. Understanding and appreciation of the 18th Vow of Amida Buddha is the essence of Jodo Shinshu Buddhism.

V. Vasubandhu is the Sanskrit name for the Indian master, *Tenjin*.

W. Wisteria in a hanging position is the official crest of the Jodo Shinshu Hongwanji-ha.

X. X plus X encircled makes the Wheel of Dharma, which illustrates the Eightfold Path.

Y. Yuien was the faithful disciple of Shinran Shonin, who is considered to be the author of *Tanni-sho*.

Z. Zenran was the unfortunate eldest son of Shinran Shonin, who did not follow his father's instructions of the Nembutsu teachings.

The Commencement Ceremony and "Ojo" (Birth into the Pure Land)

June is the month of graduations, and also the month of Father's Day Sunday. I still remember a few Dharma talks that my late father delivered. He was a minister of the Hawaii Betsuin in Honolulu when the Japanese Imperial Navy attacked Pearl Harbor on Sunday, December 7, 1941. He had Sunday services in the morning at the Betsuin. But that night, he and other ministers were picked up and brought to the Honolulu jail for questioning by FBI agents. Then he was interned on the mainland of the United States, and later was sent back to Japan in an exchange of internees between the United States and Japan.

One of his Dharma talks that I still remember clearly was about the meaning of *Sotsugyo*, a Japanese term for graduation, and *Ojo*, or Birth into the Pure Land in Buddhism. *Sotsugyo* in Japanese means the completion of one's studies, whereas in English we refer to the graduation ceremony as a "commencement," which means "to begin." As a young boy in Japan, I thought that the English expression was very interesting. I listened closely to my father's Dharma talk.

My father compared the commencement ceremony to the Buddhist expression of death. He said that death in Buddhism is not the end of our eternal lives, but it is *Ojo* or "Birth into the Pure Land." It is the beginning of a new life as the Buddha, the Enlightened One, the Compassionate One.

Jodo Shinshu Buddhism teaches that we will all be born into the Pure Land to become the Buddha after we die. The development of Jodo Shinshu Buddhism can be traced historically to three types of learning in Buddhism: precept (*sila*), meditation (*samadhi*), and wisdom (*prajna*).

By practicing the three types of learning, ordinary people gradually realize the difficulty of practicing the precepts and meditation in order to attain the state of enlightenment. From the realization of this difficulty arose Mahayana Buddhism, to provide more suitable guidance on the path to enlightenment. Mahayana means "Large (*Maha*) Vehicle (*yana*)." Thus, Mahayana Buddhism is the teaching that can carry more people to the state of enlightenment. The Bodhisattva ideal became the most important characteristic of Mahayana Buddhism, because the Bodhisattva works primarily for others for the Bodhisattva's own benefit. The Bodhisattva Dharmakara became Amida Buddha by fulfilling forty-eight Vows in order to lead all sentient beings to enlightenment. Then, Amida Buddha established his Pure Land, where sentient beings are born to become the Buddha.

When Father's Day comes, I recall my late father, and I realize that his Dharma talk is still alive in my heart. The following is a favorite poem that reminds me of my late father's Dharma talk:

Even though parents are gone,
The compassionate hearts of parents will continue
to remain
In blessing the child to become a truthful person.

Global Obon, It's Festival Day

One day, I was invited to the *Otoki* dinner at a Chinese restaurant, following a memorial service. As usual, fortune cookies were served at the end of the meal. I took one and opened it to read this saying:

"Mothers are the only goddesses in whom the whole world believes."

When I read this saying, I realized that people around the whole world respect and love their mothers. The origin of

Obon is based on the *Ullambana Sutra*, which describes the beautiful thought of Moggallana, one of the ten great disciples of Shakyamuni Buddha, and his mother.

The story of Obon tells us about an affectionate son, Moggallana, who saved his mother from the realm of suffering. This story was well received in China and Japan, as well as the United States and elsewhere in the world, because it describes the warmth of a mother's love and her relationship to her child. I could not help but recall this Obon story when I read the above fortune cookie's saying.

When Moggallana asked Shakyamuni Buddha how to save his mother from the realm of suffering, Shakyamuni Buddha advised Moggallana to practice unselfish giving (pure *dana*). When Moggallana followed Shakyamuni Buddha's advice, his mother was relieved from the realm of suffering. As Moggallana saw this, he danced around joyously. This became the origin of Bon dancing.

It is true that a mother is the first and foremost person to take care of one's life, and who all human beings love and respect. The *Ullambana Sutra* also reminds people to recollect in gratitude our departed parents and ancestors, who laid the foundations of our lives.

On October 1, 2004, when Ichiro Suzuki of the Seattle Mariners set the major-league record for hits in a season with 259, breaking George Sisler's 84-year-old mark at Safeco Field in Seattle, a reporter of the *Mainichi Shinbun* in Japan asked about the great achievement of his son, Ichiro. Mr. Nobuyuki Suzuki, Ichiro's father, replied:

"I wish to thank my ancestors for giving me Ichiro!"

The response of Ichiro's father, published online in the *Mainichi Shinbun*, conveys his deep appreciation for his ancestors and the happiness that they had given him.

According to Jodo Shinshu Buddhist tradition, Obon is also called *Kangi-e* or "A Gathering of Joy." The word *Kangi* consists of two Chinese characters, both having the meanings "joy" or "happiness." Shinran Shonin explained this term in his main writing, *Kyogyoshinsho* (*Teaching, Practice, Awakening, and Enlightenment*), by stating that "*Kangi* expresses joy and happiness in body and mind."

Obon is a great opportunity to reflect upon our ancestors, the roots of our family trees, and to meet with loved ones in joy and happiness. The Buddhist Obon observance is truly a global festival day!

Obon: Reflection on Motherhood

Karaoke is a Japanese word, which means "orchestra music without a song." Karaoke became so popular in Japan in the late 1970s that there are now Karaoke rooms in many restaurants, even in the United States. People enjoy the beautiful and artistic expressions of Japanese *Kayokyoku* songs with Karaoke accompaniment. Some *Kayokyoku* songs express the heart of the Japanese people, while others describe their dreams and inspirations. Some *Kayokyoku* songs may be considered Japanese art, while others may rise to the level of a religious awakening. One of the reasons that Karaoke has become so popular in Japan is because they are such beautiful songs.

Over thirty-five years ago, the song, *Ofukuro-san*, by the singer Shinichi Mori, became very popular. The Japanese word *Ofukuro-san* means "Mother" or "Mom" in English. The words of the song are very inspirational, starting with the following words:

> *Ofukuro-san yo! Ofukuro-san, when I look up at the sky, you are in the sky…*
> *Ofukuro-san yo! Ofukurosan, when I look at the flowers, you are in the flowers…*
> *Ofukuro-san yo! Ofukuro-san, when I look at the mountains, you are in the mountains…*

When I listen to this song, I think about how wonderful the songwriter's mother was to have raised him. His reflection on his mother is great literature, and it reaches even to the realm of religion. Later, I learned that he was the relative of a Jodo Shinshu Buddhist minister in Hiroshima Prefecture, Japan.

When a person looks up at the sky, or a person looks at flowers, or a person looks toward the mountains, reflecting upon their own mother, she appears in whatever the person is seeing.

In Jodo Shinshu Buddhism, Amida Buddha is often addressed as *Oya-sama* (parent). Amida Buddha means Infinite Life and Infinite Light. This means that Amida Buddha is always anywhere and in any time.

When Obon season comes, people often recall their own mothers. The story of Obon reminds us about the affectionate son, Moggallana (*Mokuren-sonjya*), who saved his mother from the realm of suffering. This story describes a mother's love and her relationship to her child.

The most impressive part of the *Ofukuro-san* song is that the three verses of the song end with a pledge, "I will not forget the truth of your words." On the occasion of Obon, it would be nice if everyone could tell their own mother, "I will not forget the truth of your words."

Fall Ohigan

-The Land of Utmost Happiness-

Ohigan in Japanese is an abbreviation of *To-Higan*, which literally means, "to reach the other shore." The "O" of *Ohigan* is an honorific prefix. The Buddhist term for *Ohigan* in Sanskrit is *Paramita*, which means "gone to the other shore; crossed, transcend; coming or leading to the opposite shore, complete attainment, perfection..." (from the *Monier-Williams' Sanskrit-English Dictionary*, p. 619). In Buddhism, the world of birth and death (Samsara) is referred to as "this shore," while the world of perfection (Nirvana) is called "the other shore." Therefore, Ohigan means to cross over to the other shore of the Buddha, from this shore of the mundane world.

The *Smaller Sukhavativyuha Sutra* describes the Land of the Buddha, the Land of Utmost Happiness, and the way in which people living in this world of turmoil can reach it. This sutra is one of the three principal sutras of Jodo Shinshu Buddhism. The Sanskrit term *Sukhavati* was translated into Chinese in 402 A.D. by Tripitaka Master Kumarajiva of Yao Ch'in as Gokuraku, which means "Utmost Happiness" in English. In the *Larger* and *Smaller Sukhavativyuha Sutras,* two of the three principal sutras of Jodo Shinshu Buddhism, the Land of Utmost Happiness is described illustriously with descriptions that are both artistic and religious. However, for those who do not have any insight into religious awakening, these descriptions of the Land of Utmost Happiness are understood almost as if they are the setting for a fairy story.

The *Smaller Sukhavativyuha Sutra* states that "From here to the direction of the west, beyond ten billion Buddha-lands, there is a land called the Utmost Happiness. In that land there is a Buddha named Infinite Light (*Amitabha*). He is now, at present, preaching the Dharma." During the long history of Pure Land Buddhism, the Land of Utmost Happiness has been expounded and commented upon by the Seven Masters and Shinran Shonin.

The Second Master, Vasubandhu, stated in his commentary, *The Discourse on the Pure Land*, that "I take refuge in the Buddha of Unhindered Light and I wish to be born in the Pure Land of the Buddha." Master Vasubandhu described twenty-nine adornments of the Land of Utmost Happiness, which he summarized into three categories: seventeen adornments of the Land of the Buddha, eight adornments of the Amitabha (*Amida*) Buddha, and four adornments of the Bodhisattvas. He explained that Dharma-nature is a virtue of the adornment of Purity, the

One Dharma Phrase. Then, he concluded the perfection of the twenty-nine adornments, in the three categories, into the One Dharma Phrase of "Purity."

The Third Master, T'an-luan, used the expression of "the Pure Land" in his *Commentary on the Discourse on the Pure Land*. He replaced "the Land of Utmost Happiness (*Gokuraku*)" with the term "Pure Land (*Jodo*)." Thus, among the Seven Masters of Jodo Shinshu Buddhism, Master T'an-luan was the first to use the term "Pure Land" (*Jodo*) for Land of Utmost Happiness (*Gokuraku*). His intention was to expound upon the true meaning of the Land of the Buddha. His presentation of the Pure Land is considered to be the demythologization of the Land of Utmost Happiness.

The observance of the Ohigan service is to understand the true meaning of the other shore of the Buddha, the Land of Purity and Compassion, which everyone is encouraged to reach.

Eitaikyo

-Perpetual Memorial Service-

Eitaikyo is the Perpetual Memorial Service for the deceased. This is an annual observance for Buddhists, in which they reflect on the dedicated lives of the deceased and express their appreciation through the Nembutsu. During the service, it is natural to think about such questions as "Where do we go after we die?" or "What will happen after death?"

The Seattle Betsuin Buddhist Church hosted the 2008 Northwest District Buddhist Convention with the theme of "Come Home to the Nembutsu," or *Nembutsu ni Kaeru* in Japanese. The Japanese word *Kaeru* has two meanings—one is "come back" and the other is "frog." So, a frog was chosen as the logo for the convention.

Although the idea for the theme was submitted in an anonymous note, it was extremely impressive, both heartwarming and representative of the essence of Jodo Shinshu Buddhism.

The author of this theme stated in the note, "how wonderful to be able to say that our temple, Sangha, and the Nembutsu are like home, where we can always come home." The author showed a wonderful understanding of Jodo Shinshu Buddhism, with a sense of humor. It is great to say that the Nembutsu, Namo Amida Butsu, is my home, where I will always return.

Shinran stated in his main writing, *Kyogyoshinsho (Teaching, Practice, Awakening Faith, and Enlightenment)*, the following:

> *Reverently contemplating the true essence of Jodo Shinshu Buddhism, I see that Amida Buddha's directing of virtue to sentient beings has two aspects: the aspect for our going forth to the Pure Land of Amida Buddha and the aspect for our returning to this world.*

Shinran also expressed these aspects of coming and going in a statement on his final day:

> *Even though I go to the Pure Land after my earthly life ended, I will go back and forth to this world to spread the compassion of Amida Buddha just like the high waves that constantly flow back and forth in the Bay of Waka.*

We find that Shinran's going to the Pure Land, when he died, was also his coming home to the Pure Land. The author of the 2008 Convention theme understood Shinran's teaching, restating it as "Coming Home to the Nembutsu."

Some readers may ask, "Is saying the Nembutsu the way to the Pure Land?" To answer this, I wish to follow a famous Buddhist scholar, Dr. Daisetz T. Suzuki, who said that there are two approaches to understanding the Pure Land of Amida Buddha: one is to understand the original purpose of the Pure Land, and the other is to understand the function of the original purpose of the Pure Land. The original purpose of the Pure Land is nothing but to show the Primal Vow of Amida Buddha whose essence is compassion.

When one is awakened to the Primal Vow of Amida Buddha, one finds the function of such compassion in the Nembutsu. It is wonderful to know that the author of the convention's theme has reminded us that the Nembutsu, Namo Amida Butsu, is the compassion of the Pure Land, a place where everyone can come home.

Bodhi Day

-Day of Enlightenment-

Siddhartha Gautama was born in India more than 2,500 years ago as the Prince of the Kingdom of Kapilavastu. There is a legendary story of his excursions from the four gates of his castle that took place before he renounced his royal life and became a monk, a seeker of the truth.

Traveling from the four gates of east, west, south, and north, he witnessed sickness, old age, death, and a peacefully meditating monk. He realized that sickness, old age, and death are suffering in our lives. He realized also that by the sheer nature of being born, life itself is suffering. Thus, he discovered that birth, old age, sickness, and death are the four kinds of suffering in our human lives. He abandoned his worldly position and pleasures at the age of twenty-nine to seek the cause of suffering and a way to true happiness.

In order to find true happiness, Siddhartha observed ascetic practices of self-discipline for six years. He found, however, that he had made no progress toward extinguishing suffering. So, he gave up his ascetic practices, seeing them as useless. Abandoning both luxurious and ascetic lives, he decided to meditate under the Pippala tree to find the truth of life. (The Pippala tree was renamed the Bodhi tree after Siddhartha became an Enlightened One under that tree.) He sat there for 49 days. According to the Mahayana tradition, he attained the Highest Enlightenment in the early morning of December 8, at the age of 35, thus becoming the Buddha, the Enlightened One. The highest state of enlightenment is expressed as the "Unexcelled Perfect Enlightenment (*Anuttara Samyak Sambodhi*)" in the Buddhist Scriptures.

His enlightenment was the realization of the Doctrine of Interdependency (Pratityasamutpada). The formula of this doctrine is expressed as follows:

From the existence of this, that becomes;
From the happening of this, that happens.
From the non-existence of this, that does not become;
From the non-existence of this, that does not happen.

This formula teaches us how everything exists interdependently. This became one of the most important teachings for our lives. We are all living our lives interdependently. This realization of interdependency led to the Japanese expression of *Okage-sama* (I am indebted to you and other numerous conditions. How grateful I am).

The *Salistamba Sutra* states that everyone sees the Buddha and the truth of life by realizing the Doctrine of Interdependency.

Whosoever sees the Doctrine of Interdependency sees the Buddha;
Whoever sees the Buddha sees the Truth of life.

Buddhists celebrate the day of the Buddha's Enlightenment as Bodhi Day or *Jodo-e* (Fulfillment of One's Path). Furthermore, the teaching of the Buddha is guiding millions of people throughout the world today. We should be grateful for our family and friends and the opportunity to learn the Buddha Dharma. Let us all celebrate Bodhi Day with gratitude.

Gold Medalist Kristi Yamaguchi

(Photograph Courtesy of Kristi Yamaguchi)

Chapter IV- GRATEFUL KARMIC ASSOCIATIONS

Gold Medalist Kristi Yamaguchi

"Why should people attend Dharma School?"
"What do people learn at Dharma School?"
"What benefit do people get by attending Dharma School?"

Being involved in a Dharma School program, it is inevitable that we hear these questions from the Buddhist Sangha, and even from ourselves. The above questions can only be answered by reflecting on aspects of human life, as taught by Buddhism.

Question I – Direction and Goal in Life

The question "Why should people attend Dharma School (or by extension, a Buddhist service)?" corresponds religiously to the question "Why are people living?" It is essential for people to have a definite direction in their lives. Dr. Yuichi Kajiyama talks in his book, *The Meaning of Bodhisattva*, about a Japanese *Rakugo*, a comic story, which was influenced by Buddhism. In this *Rakugo* story, a father is scolding his son, who spends his days fooling around and sleeping. The following conversation takes place between the father and the son:

Father: "Hey! Don't sleep all the time. Wake up for a while and study!"
Son: "What will happen if I study?"
Father: "You can get into a good university."
Son: "What will happen if I go to a good university?"
Father: "You can get a good job."
Son: "What will happen if I get a good job?"
Father: "You can make lots of money and become rich.

Then you can have a comfortable life, so that you can lead a life of sleep."
Son: "That's why I am sleeping now."

This story reminds us of the importance of having a real goal in our lives. When I was assigned to the Southern Alameda County Buddhist Church in California in 1982, I met a cute little ten-year-old girl in the Dharma School. Her name was Kristi Yamaguchi. She happened to be the same age as my youngest son, Hugh.

By that time, she had already begun ice-skating, and was showing indications of becoming a serious competitor. She spent the next ten years of her life training, getting up 3:30 every morning to practice at the ice rink.

During those early years, she received many awards, including the 1988 World Junior Championship and the 1991 World Championship. Finally, on February 21, 1992, at the XVI Winter Olympics in Albertville, France, Kristi captured the Gold Medal in Women's Figure Skating.

When I reflect upon her life over the past ten years, I have nothing but great respect for her tenacity and drive to set forth her goal and move forward with it. I also admire her parents, Dr. and Mrs. Jim Yamaguchi, for their guidance and support in her endeavors.

Now, it is nice that everyone should have their own goals to follow. For example, Buddhism is called *Butsudo* or the path of the Buddha, just as *Kado* is the path of the flower, *Sado* is the path of tea, *Kendo* is the path of the sword, and *Judo* is the path of softness. Buddhism teaches this path as a direction to the goal of enlightenment, under the guiding light of the Buddha. Dharma School is there to help people find direction and to set goals in their lives. This is the main reason why people should attend Dharma School.

Question II – What do people learn at Dharma School?

What do people learn at Dharma School? If I were to respond, "We learn that our life is difficult," many children will probably say, "That's why I don't go to Dharma School." To that, I would respond with another story about Kristi. After receiving the Gold Medal, Kristi appeared on the Arsenio Hall Show on March 5, 1992. Arsenio asked Kristi about a rough spot in her routine during the Olympics. He asked her, "You put your hand down on the ice, but got up and continued. How were you able to recover and perform the way you did?" Kristi responded, "Definitely it's a part of my training. When we are practicing ... when we make a mistake, we go on with it."

I found her statement to be very Buddhistic. Kristi described how her training does not only involve her just going out and performing the beautiful leaps and twists that we see on television; but it also deals with the hardships that she endures in preparing for those routines.

Buddha taught that life is difficult. His message was that life is not easy, and that people must learn how to deal with that fact. People must go on with their lives, despite the many difficulties that they must endure. This is one of the important teachings that people may learn at Dharma School.

Question III – What benefit do people get by attending Dharma School?

One month after winning the Gold Medal, Kristi participated in the 1992 World Figure Skating Championships, and she defended her title at the Oakland Coliseum. The Coliseum was packed with over 14,000 spectators. Finishing in first place on the first day of the performances, she was asked by a reporter of the San Francisco Examiner how she could skate so beautifully. She replied, "I was using the energy of the crowd to give me more excitement on the ice." Receiving that energy from over 14,000 enthusiastic fans, she performed in a state of "No-Mind," or "Oneness with Others."

Thus, to answer the question "What benefit do people get by attending Dharma School?," I would like people to think of Kristi once again. Buddhists learn that they are all embraced by the energy of their parents' love and the energy of the

Compassion of Amida Buddha. People learn about that energy of the Great Compassion and Wisdom at Dharma School. This is the benefit that people get by attending Dharma School.

In order for children to grow up with dreams and hope, it is very important for them to attend Dharma School.

Astronaut Ellison Onizuka

(Photograph Courtesy of NASA and Lorna Onizuka)

Astronaut Ellison Onizuka: Memorial Speech

-39th Annual Northwest District Buddhist Convention Spokane, Washington, February 15, 1986-

I feel greatly honored and privileged to be before you a speaker at the 39th Annual Buddhist Convention. At the same time, however, I feel great sadness and sorrow, and even disappointment, as all of you feel, because we were anxious to listen to the first Japanese-American and Shin Buddhist to become an astronaut. Under unfortunate circumstances, I feel very sorry to take over the duty as principal speaker for the convention, in place of the late Lt. Col. Ellison Onizuka. I had originally agreed to take over this duty, if his mission, which was scheduled to lift-off on January 21, was delayed and NASA could not release him for the convention. I never expected such a tragedy, yet in the early morning on Tuesday, January 28, millions of people around the world were plunged into deep sadness when the Space Shuttle Challenger exploded in the air 73 seconds after lift-off at Cape Canaveral, killing all seven crew members, including our Ellison.

Regardless of whether we knew the crew members or not, their deaths moved us greatly. They touched our hearts as pioneers and heroes. Ellison's death had touched all of us in a personal way; he was the first American of Japanese ancestry to reach the dream that many thought impossible; to become an astronaut and the first Jodo Shinshu Buddhist to enter space. I would like to dedicate my speech to Lt. Col. Ellison Onizuka and share with you his personal life; a life which had all the markings of a leader and an outstanding Buddhist.

I became a resident minister at the Kona Hongwanji Mission on the island of Hawaii on September of 1962. Ellison's parents, Mr. and Mrs. Masamitsu Onizuka, were active in the Mission. His father encouraged Ellison to get an education and to make something of himself. He died on February 20, 1968, a month before Ellison graduated from the University of Colorado. It was evident that his father's inspiration always remained in Ellison's heart. After becoming an astronaut, he often said, "I wish my father and grandfather could see me."

Ellison, while attending Konawaena High School, was president of the Junior Young Buddhists Association. As president, I can remember Ellison always demonstrated good leadership, during which time the Kona Junior YBA hosted the Hawaii United Conference. He had a deep sense of respect for the Buddha, his parents, and teachers, and was well-liked and respected by his peers. Outside of church, Ellison was student-body president of Konawaena High School. He played varsity baseball and basketball, serving as captain of the baseball team. He was also active in the Boy Scouts, becoming an Eagle Scout, as well as president of the state 4-H Federation in Hawaii. As a 4-H representative, he attended the national conference in Washington, DC, in 1963.

After I was transferred to the Sacramento Betsuin Buddhist Church, from Hawaii, we had an opportunity to meet Ellison for the first time in 17 years at McClellan Air Force Base, when my wife and I were invited to attend the Asian-Pacific American Heritage Week banquet in 1981, where Ellison was the principal speaker. After he returned to NASA, he wrote, "It's been a while since I used to attend the Kona Hongwanji; but all of what I learned there has not been forgotten. Thank you for all that you have done to help me through those influential years." One of the most gratifying moments is to see people who were brought up in the Buddhist tradition become responsible and productive citizens, who live and practice truly as Buddhists, in gratitude and Gassho. After the tragedy of Challenger, Japanese television broadcast a segment in which Ellison was shown, with his mother, wife, and children, visiting Fukuoka Prefecture in 1983 to pay respects at the Onizuka family's ancestral gravesite, each holding an Ojuzu in their hands. Ms. Sodetani, a writer, wrote of this scene, "Ellison wanted to pay his respects. It is an arresting image, for while the astronaut's hands touched quietly in meditation, his gaze had a depth of intensity unlike any other. What's going through his mind, one wonders, as he faces the tomb, hearing his father's—his own—family name? What kind of connection inspires this look?"

Ellison wrote, "The many sacrifices of the *Issei* and *Nisei* to overcome once unbelievable obstacles with honor, pride, and hard work—their dedication and tradition have given all of us a very special heritage to build on. You must not forget the dream, the sacrifices, and the path-finding of the generations before us . . . try to make them proud."

All of these words and actions reflected his outlook on life. He lived in gratitude to all the people who made his life possible. As a result, he truly lived with pride as an American of Japanese ancestry and of Buddhist faith, fighting against the odds as a minority in both. He was a true gentleman of Buddhist faith, sharing his warm, friendly, and compassionate heart with everyone he met, and died as a pioneer astronaut for all the people in the world. We all truly miss him.

Although we are not able to see him physically anymore, the memory of his gentle smile will give us a feeling of confidence and pride in our heritage. His great achievement as an astronaut, as well as Jodo Shinshu Buddhist, will serve as an example for all of us. May his contributions to science and society be an inspiration to us, our children, grandchildren, and many generations to come. Namo Amida Butsu.

Atomic Bomb Victims' Memorial

The Atomic Bomb was dropped over Hiroshima City on August 6, 1945, killing over 100,000 people. Three days later, on August 9, another Atomic Bomb was dropped over Nagasaki City, killing over 70,000 people.

I discovered that one of the winning Haikus in the 2006 NHK All-Japan Haiku Contest was about Hiroshima City. It reads,

Hiroshima wa
Imamo Hiroshima
Kumono-mine

A Haiku is a short poem of seventeen syllables that turns a significant intuition into a statement of reality. Dr. Daisetz T. Suzuki, a distinguished Buddhist scholar stated in his book, Zen and Japanese Culture, that "it is impossible to speak of Japanese culture apart from Buddhism, for in every phase of its development, we recognized the presence of Buddhist feeling in one way or another."

Dr. R. H. Blyth, an authority on the study of Haiku in English, also states in his book, Zen in English Literature and Oriental Classics, that "The Haiku is not merely descriptive, it is of religious connotation."

I appreciated very much the winning Haiku of the 2006 contest about Hiroshima, since it reminded me of three periods of our history, past, present, and future. When I read the line, "Hiroshima wa," I recalled August 6, 1945. I was only an 11-year-old boy, living on the other side of the mountain range from Hiroshima City in Shimane Prefecture. Some of the people in my village saw a flash of light in the sky above the mountains. Later, my junior high school graduation trip visited Hiroshima City, where we stood under the skeleton-domed building under where the Atomic Bomb was detonated. In those days, the city allowed us to go into that building.

Overcoming all difficulties and hardship, Hiroshima has recovered beautifully today. I find the second line of 7 syllables, "Imamo Hiroshima," speaks of how Hiroshima recovered and became a symbol of peace.

The third line of 5 syllables, "Kumo no Mine," inspires us to seek a bright future of "Hope" and "Awakening." The Japanese phrase "Kumo no Mine" means "a gigantic column of clouds" in English. The author of this Haiku poem saw beautiful clouds, which extended far up into the sky. He did not see the clouds of the Atomic Bomb, known as the "Mushroom Cloud." He only saw beautiful clouds in the sky of Hiroshima City. This Haiku truly reminds us that there will be a bright and inspiring future for Hiroshima City.

After I retired as Rimban from the Seattle Betsuin Buddhist Temple in July 2010, I served as the resident minister of the New York Buddhist Church from October 2010 to December 2012.

The New York Buddhist Church is located at 105th Street and Riverside Drive in Manhattan, New York. The historic, five-storied building faces the Hudson River. And in front of the church is a huge bronze statue of Shinran Shonin.

That statue is different from other Shinran Shonin statues because it was a victim of the Atomic Bomb, which was dropped on Hiroshima City on August 6, 1945. The statue still has red burn marks on the body. The statue was donated to the New York Buddhist Church by Mr. Seiichi Hirose, a successful businessman and a devout Jodo Shinshu Buddhist follower from Hiroshima, as a symbol for world peace.

The statue was unveiled on September 11, 1955; and the keynote speaker at the dedication ceremony was the famous Buddhist scholar, Dr. Daisetz T. Suzuki, who happened to be a visiting professor at Columbia University at the time. Columbia University is located very near to the New York Buddhist Church.

Dr. D. T. Suzuki quoted a Koan story in his speech, which was recorded by the American Buddhist Study Center as follows:

> *Many years ago there was, in China, a great Buddhist government officer. He, one day, visited a Buddhist temple. When he was ushered by the monks into a room where a number of portraits were hung on the wall, he pointed out one of them and asked, "Who is this?"*
>
> *A monk replied: "A portrait of the late abbot."*
>
> *"Portrait is here, but where is the person?"*
>
> *Nobody was able to answer the question, but the officer was persistent. Finding, however, no one proceeding to satisfy him, he finally said:*
>
> *"In this big monastery there must be someone who can answer my question. Won't you try to hunt someone up?"*
>
> *They happened to think of one of the monks who quite recently joined them, "He is at present working in the garden, but he seems very likely to be the one who can answer such a question as you propose."*
>
> *He was brought in.*
>
> *The high officer politely said, "There is a question I wish very much to have answered. But these gentlemen about here are not disposed toward giving me satisfaction. Will you be good enough to do me a great favor?"*
>
> *The gardener-monk said, "What is your question?"*
>
> *The officer, pointing at the picture said, "I am told that this is the portrait of the abbot who recently passed away. I want to know where the person is at this moment."*
>
> *The monk called out, "O Governor!" The officer at once responded, "Yes, reverend sir." The monk lost no time in giving this message to him:*
>
> *"Here is the person quite fully alive."*

Since this was the quotation of a Koan story, Dr. Suzuki did not give any explanation of the gardener-monk's answer. But we may be able to come up with several interpretations. For example, the governor was a faithful follower of the late abbot; or the gardener-monk was a distinguished Buddhist.

At the end of his speech, Dr. Suzuki concluded with a Koan-like question:

"O Shinran Shonin, here is your statue; and where are you?"

For Dr. Suzuki's question, Shinran Shonin reminded us in his writing, "If you are alone, think you are two. If you are two, think you are three. Other is Shinran!"

I can also raise a similar question, "We are observing a memorial service for the Atomic Bomb victims; and where are our loved ones?"

Jodo Shinshu Buddhism gives us an answer with the Nembutsu (Think about the Buddha), Namo Amida Butsu. In it I find the compassionate heart of our loved ones.

Jodo Shinshu Buddhism also teaches that those who pass away before us are good teachers, who taught us physically that "Our life is impermanent." Therefore, it is important to live meaningfully at this moment.

Rennyo Shonin reminded us in his letter that "In the morning, we may have radiant health; but in the evening, we may return to white ashes."

Lady Takeko Kujo, daughter of His Eminence the 21st Monshu Koson Ohtani of the Hongwanji, taught us beautifully in her Buddhist Gatha, *Seiya*, where in the second verse, she writes, "More numerous than the sands of the Ganges River are the Buddhas, who are watching over us day and night. When I hear this, my heart becomes peaceful."

Jodo Shinshu Buddhism teaches us that we are always embraced by the Great Compassion and Wisdom of the Buddha.

Gotan-e: Birthday of the Great Religious Leader Shinran Shonin

-CBS Nationwide Broadcast of "Meeting Place: Canadians at Worship," Vancouver Buddhist Temple, April 30, 1995.-

We are observing the Gotan-e service to commemorate the birthday of Shinran Shonin, the founder of Jodo Shinshu Buddhism. Shinran was born on May 21, 1173, near Kyoto, Japan. Jodo Shinshu Buddhism is one of the two major Buddhist traditions, Mahayana Buddhism, which have spread from India, China, Korea, and Japan.

The Buddhist Churches of Canada (presently the Jodo Shinshu Buddhist Temples of Canada) was established in Vancouver, Canada, in 1905. This year marks the 90th anniversary of that founding. However, its history, from 1905 to the present, has not always been an easy one. But today the BCC churches are well-established in many major cities throughout Canada.

The famous Buddhist scholar, Dr. Daisetz T. Suzuki, once said that "The Japanese may not have offered very many original ideas to world thought or world culture; but in Japanese Shin (Jodo Shinshu Buddhism) we find a major contribution that the Japanese have made to the outside world and all the other Buddhist schools." He further stated, "Of all the developments that Mahayana Buddhism has achieved in the Far East, the most remarkable is the Shin teaching of the Pure Land School. It is remarkable chiefly because, geographically, its birthplace is Japan and, historically, it is the latest evolution of Pure Land Mahayana, and therefore the highest point it has reached."

The idea of *Jodo* or Pure Land first grew in India and developed in China during the Tang dynasty of the 6th and 7th centuries. Buddhism was first introduced to Japan, from China, in the middle of the 6th century. But in those days Buddhism

Kenshin - Revealing the Truth

was an aristocratic religion; and entrance into the Buddhist monasteries was restricted to noble people, isolating them from the ordinary people. Buddhism was well accepted in Japan and very highly developed in its Japanese form during the Kamakura period of the 12th and 13th centuries. During that time, Shinran founded *Jodo Shinshu* or True Pure Land Buddhism. Shinran had a profound understanding of the human nature of an ordinary person and the great compassion of Amida Buddha.

One of the most important characteristics of Mahayana Buddhism is the Bodhisattva ideal, in which one works for others for one's own benefit. Shinran taught that Amida Buddha is always extending his great compassion and wisdom to all people. This is the function of the Primal Vow of Amida Buddha. The Primal Vow assures us that all beings will be led to enlightenment by awakening to the great compassion and wisdom of Amida Buddha. The universal compassionate heart of Amida Buddha was described in the *Tanni-sho* (*Notes Lamenting Differences*) by Shinran's disciple in a rather unique way. It states that "Even a good person is born in the Pure Land, how much more so is an evil person. However, people in the world usually say, 'Even an evil person is born in the Pure Land, how much more so is a good person.' At first sight this view seems to be reasonable, but it is contrary to the purport of the Primal Vow of Amida Buddha."

A book about the history of Japanese-Canadians, entitled *One Hundred Year History of the Canadian Immigration*, describes the life of a Japanese immigrant, Mrs. Fude Nakatsu, who was born in Wakayama Prefecture in Japan, who married Yasutaro Nakatsu in Canada in 1916, when she was 26 years old. She states that her mother's last words at the time of her departure from Japan were, "Fude, I will send you off from home; but when you miss your father and mother, please recite Namo Amida Butsu." Namo Amida Butsu means "I take refuge in the great compassion and wisdom of Amida Buddha." Shinran reminds us that we are always embraced by the great compassion and wisdom of Amida Buddha, even though we are living through hardships and loneliness. His unique expression in the *Tanni-sho* reminds us that all beings, regardless there status, are the subjects of Amida Buddha's concern, just as parents are concerned about their children.

In the 90-year history of the Buddhist Churches of Canada, the Japanese immigrants of the early period of immigration to Canada were able to overcome their difficulties, discriminations, and sorrow by awakening and rejoicing in the great compassion of Amida Buddha. In spite of such difficult living conditions, they pursued their high moral standard with the guidance of Amida Buddha's great wisdom.

Shinran taught that the Nembutsu, Namo Amida Butsu, means oneness with the great compassion and wisdom of Amida Buddha. He also taught that a life of the Nembutsu is a true way of life. The *Tanni-sho* (*Notes Lamenting Differences*) states, "A life of the Nembutsu, Namo Amida Butsu, is an Unimpeded Single Path."

When Shinran taught about the life of the Nembutsu, Namo Amida Butsu, to the ordinary people, he was exiled to the northern country of Japan by the Japanese government. He was the first Buddhist priest to lead a married and ordinary family life in public. He partook in regular meals that included fresh meat. He emphasized that the Primal Vow of Amida Buddha does not discriminate against anyone because of their social or physical conditions or lifestyle. And he declared himself as neither monk nor layman.

He rejoiced in writing, "When I carefully consider the Primal Vow which Amida Buddha brought forth, I find that it was only for me, Shinran, alone! How gracious is the Primal Vow of Amida Buddha, who resolved to lead me to enlightenment." He taught us that the true way to enlightenment is the way of the Nembutsu, Namo Amida Butsu.

After Shinran passed away on January 16, 1262, and as time went on, Shinran's real character and teachings were truly recognized in Japan. Jodo Shinshu Buddhism developed to be one of the largest Buddhist denominations today. And in November 1876, six hundred and fourteen years after Shinran's death, the Emperor Meiji of Japan presented him with a special title, *Kenshin Daishi* or "The Great Teacher who has revealed the Truth."

As we celebrate Shinran's birthday, we appreciate his dedicated religious guidance.

Contemporary Understanding of the Pure Land of Utmost Bliss

-14th Biennial Conference of the International Association of Shin Buddhist Studiers, Ryukoku University, Kyoto, Japan, June 14th 2009-

(1)

It is very important to present and explain the Pure Land of Utmost Bliss, one of the basic doctrines of Jodo Shinshu Buddhism, to modern people. The *Smaller Pure Land Sutra* (*Sukhavativyuha*, 仏説阿弥陀経) states that the location of the Land of Utmost Bliss is "From here to the west, beyong ten billion Buddha-lands, there is a world called the Land of Utmost Bliss (*Sukhavati* or *Gokuraku*)."[1] (従是西方過十万億仏土有世界名曰極楽) Then, the Land of Utmost Bliss is described as follows:

> *"... there are seven rows of balconies, seven rows of fine nets, and seven rows of Palmyra trees. All these are decorated with four kinds of jewels that surround and encircle the country. ... there exists the pond of seven jewels, filled completely with water of the eight kinds of virtues. The inside of the pond, at the bottom, is covered exclusively with gold sands."*[2]
>
> 七重欄楯 七重羅網 七重行樹 皆是四宝周帀囲繞・・・有七宝池 八功徳水 充満其中 池底純以 金沙布地

Descriptions of the Land of Utmost Bliss, as found in the three Pure Land Sutras (浄土三部経), particularly the Smaller Sutra, as well as in other commentaries, are illustrious and artistic, making them very difficult for modern people to understand. Speaking of such descriptions of the Pure Land, Dr. Genpo Hoshino, a former professor of Ryukoku University, stated in his book, entitled "Pure Land" (浄土), that "For those who are seeking the logic of the establishment of the Pure Land, these descriptions may seem only to be the account of a dream, particularly for us modern people; and such descriptions are boring. Yet, I believe that, because of the perceived boredom of these descriptions, the Pure Land needs to be reviewed seriously by modern society. Though this task will be difficult and uninteresting to some, it is a problem that must be tackled by modern people. It is a task that cannot be left alone."[3]

His Eminence Monshu Koshin Ohtani also expressed his concern about a modern understanding of the Pure Land in his Dharma message entitled "The importance in having opportunities to feel the Pure Land in daily life" ("生活の中でお浄土が感じられる縁が大事"), saying "The expressions of Birth into the Pure Land (往生浄土), The Pure Land of Utmost Bliss (極楽浄土), are not being introduced gradually, and Going to Heaven (天国) or the World of Stars (星) after Death have often been expressed instead. I think that this is the great task of the basic Jodo Shinshu teachings … Is it possible to express the concepts of 'Namo Amida Butsu as Calling of Amida Buddha,' 'Scriptures in which Shakyamuni praised Amida Tathagata and his Pure Land,' and 'Shinran Shonin's Hymns of Shoshin-ge' in a way that will touch the heartstrings of modern people?"[4]

Dr. Daisetz T. Suzuki, the famous Buddhist scholar, stated that "There are two approaches to understanding the Pure Land of Amida Buddha: one is to determine the establisher's intention of the Pure Land, and the second is to determine how that intention was accomplished. The first is to approach the origin of the Pure Land, and the second is an existentialistic approach."[5] He further stated that "The origin of the Pure Land is based on the Primal Vow of Amida Buddha. The Primal Vow was established out of the great compassion (Karuna) of the Buddha's heart ... The foundation of the Pure Land is compassion. The beginning of Amida Buddha's function started with the Pure Land. Then, what is the essence of the Pure Land established by great compassion? Its essence is Enlightenment (Bodhi 正覚). By attaining Enlightenment, Amida Buddha intended to fulfill the great compassion of the Primal Vow. Therefore, the Pure Land is Enlightenment itself. To understand the characteristics, structures, and functions of the Pure Land is to understand those of Enlightenment. This is an existentialistic approach to understanding the Pure Land."[6]

(2)

In order to have a contemporary understanding of the Pure Land of Utmost Bliss, Dr. Suzuki recommended two approaches. The first approach was to determine how the Pure Land was established. Shinran Shonin defined the True Buddha and the True Buddha's Land, in his Collection of Passages Revealing the True Buddha and Land of the Pure Land Way, Vol. V (顕浄土真佛土文類五), as follows:

> *Reverently contemplating the true Buddha and the true land, I find that the Buddha is the Tathagata of inconceivable light and that the land also is the land of immeasurable light. Because they have arisen through the fulfillment of Vows of great compassion, they are called true fulfilled Buddha and land.*[7]
>
> 謹按真佛土者、仏者則是不可思議光如来、土者亦是無量光明土也。然則酬報大悲誓願故、曰真報佛土。

Shinran defined the True Buddha as the Tathagata of Inconceivable Light (不可思議光如来) and the True Land of the Buddha as the Land of Immeasurable Light (無量光明土). And the reason why Shinran defined both Buddha and his Land with the one concept of Light is that both are inseparable. Because the Buddha's Land was established through the fulfillment of Vows of the Buddha's great compassion, the Buddha's Land is also a truly fulfilled land. Shinran explained that the Buddha's Land was established as the result of the fulfillment of Vows of the Buddha's great compassion. This is the origin of the Pure Land of Utmost Bliss.

Dr. Suzuki's second, existentialistic approach was to see the function of the Pure Land of Utmost Bliss. Regarding the essence of the Pure Land of Utmost Bliss, Shinran stated in his Note on Essentials of Faith Alone (唯信鈔文意) that "The Land of Bliss is the World of Nirvana, the Uncreated,"[8] (極楽無為涅槃界), by quoting the Hojisan of Shan-tao. The World of Nirvana, the Uncreated, also means the state of Enlightenment (Bodhi).

Quoting from the definition of Shinran and other Jodo Shinshu Masters about the Pure Land of Utmost Bliss, the 2009 BCA Calendar had on its cover page:

> *Amida Buddha's Land is the Pure and Tranquil World of Nirvana.*[9]
> 仏の国土は清く安らかな涅槃の世界である

Therefore, to desire to be born into the Pure Land of Utmost Bliss is to seek to attain Nirvana and to be enlightened (Bodhi). Dr. Kyosho Hayashima, a Jodo Shinshu priest and former professor of Tokyo University, explained that the Pure Land of Utmost Bliss is the manifestation of true and real enlightenment, and to be born into the Pure Land means to seek a way to enlightenment.[10]

A famous Myokonin and devout Jodo Shinshu Buddhist, Saichi Asahara, was always enjoying the Dharma talks of Kangaku Kengyo Umeda at Anrakuji Temple in Shimane Prefecture. He composed the following poem, as a series of questions and answers to himself, about the Pure Land of Utmost Bliss.

> *"I haven't understood the Pure Land of Utmost Bliss.*
> *Where is the Pure Land?"*
> *"You are ignorant! You haven't understood the Pure Land of Utmost Bliss. You are so ignorant! The Pure Land of Utmost Bliss is nothing but Namo Amida Butsu."*

"Is that so! Oh, how grateful I am, how grateful I am!" [11]

Shinran defined the characteristic of true and real virtues of the Pure Land of Utmost Bliss as the sacred name of Namo Amida Butsu (［真実功徳］は誓願の尊号なり)[12] in his Notes on the Inscriptions on Sacred Scrolls (尊号真像銘文). The descriptions of the Pure Land of Utmost Bliss found in the three Pure Land Sutras and other commentaries are manifestations of the Vows of Amida Buddha's great compassion. Thus, Shinran expounded that the Pure Land of Utmost Bliss is the sacred name, Namo Amida Butsu, just as Saichi Asahara had appreciated in his poem.

(3)

Vasubandhu, the second Pure Land Master, wrote the *Discourse on the Pure Land* (浄土論), and with single-mindedness took refuge in the Tathagata of Unhindered Light Shining in the Ten Directions (帰命尽十方無碍光如来) and aspired to be born in the Land of Peace and Bliss (願生安楽国).

In Vasubandhu's *Discourse*, he describes the Twenty-Nine Aspects of the Virtues of the Adornments in the Three Divisions of the Buddha's Pure Land, Amida Buddha, and the Bodhisattvas (三厳二十九種功徳荘厳): seventeen adornments of the Buddha's Pure Land, eight adornments of Amida Buddha, and four adornments of the Bodhisattvas. He then expounded that these aspects could be summarized into the Phrase of One Dharma (一法句), which is the Phrase of Purity (清浄句). "The Phrase of Purity is the Uncreated Dharma Body of True and Real Wisdom (清浄句者謂真実智慧無為法身故)."[13]

Tan-luan, the third Pure Land Master, wrote the *Commentary of the Discourse on the Pure Land* (往生論註) and presented the extensive interpenetration of the Twenty-Nine Aspects of the Virtues of the Adornments in the Three Division (広) and the Phrase of One Dharma in a more condensed presentation (略). Both enter into each other because of the two types of Dharma Body. From the Essential Dharma Body (法性法身) of the Phrase of One Dharma originates the Dharma Body of Expediency (方便法身). And through the Dharma Body of

Expediency, the Essential Dharma Body is revealed. These two Dharma Bodies are different, but inseparable.

Asanga, the older brother of Vasubandhu, wrote The *Summary of the Great Vehicle (*Mahayanasamgraha, 摂大乗論) and systematically established the theory of the Tri-kaya (Three Bodies) of the Buddha in Chapter Ten, "The Distinguishing Characteristics of the Excellence of Wisdom (智差別勝相品第十)." Asanga stated that "The excellence of wisdom is to be understood as the three bodies of the Buddha, which are the essence body, the enjoyment body, and the transformation body."[14] (由仏三身応知智差別) The Essence Body (Svabhava-kaya, 自性身) is the Dharma Body (Dharma-kaya, 法身) of Tathagatas. The Enjoyment Body (Sambhoga-kaya, 受用身) is the body that is manifested in the various Buddha lands and assemblies, and enjoys the Buddha's lands and the Mahayana-dharma. The Transformation Body (Nirmana-kaya, 変化身) is also manifested in various situations in this world.

Asanga explained that there are ten meanings of the Dharma Body. The first meaning provides the five characteristics of the Dharma Body. He stated that "The Dharma Body is characterized by inconceivability, because the purity of suchness is to be known by a personal realization, because it cannot be compared to anything, and because it is beyond the scope of intelligent knowing"[15] (不可思議為相、是真如清浄自證智所知故, 無譬喩故、非覚観行処故), the fifth of the five characteristics of the Dharma body. He reminded us that the Dharma Body as the purity of suchness can be understood by a personal awakening.

In the second of the ninth meaning of the Dharma Body, Asanga presented the eighteen Perfect Purity of the Buddha's Pure Land by quoting the *One Hundred Thousand-Stanza Scripture* (百千経) as his answer to the question "How is the purity of the Pure Land of all Buddha Tathagatas to be understood?" The Scripture describes how the Pure Land came up with cause (因) and its result (果) in the 5th and 6th of the eighteen Perfect Purities. The Pure Land is perfectly purified in its cause, because "It arises from good states beyond world-transcendence.[16]

(出出世善法功能所生) And the Pure Land is perfectly purified in result, because "It is characterized by a masterfully engendered and well purified conscious construction."[17] (最清浄自在唯識為相) The 7th Perfect Purity explains that the Pure Land is the abode of the Buddha Tathagatas. (如来所鎮)

The *Summary of the Great Vehicle* expounded that the Pure Land of Utmost Bliss was originated with the good Dharma (善法) and established the numerous adornments as the manifestations (表象) from the pure consciousness (浄識) of the enlightened one. Thus, wisdom of pure consciousness of the enlightened one became the substance of the Pure Land of Utmost Bliss.[18]

Asanga's The *Summary of the Great Vehicle* and its commentaries on Vasubandhu and Asvabhava give doctrinal insight into the consciousness theory of the Yogacara School for a Contemporary Understanding of the Pure Land of Utmost Bliss.

---

1 Matsubayashi, Hoshu Y. tr. The *Sukhavativyuha Sutra*. p. 7.

2 Ibid., pp. 7-9.

3 Hoshino, Genpo. Jodo – Sonzai to Igi [Pure Land – Its Existence and Meaning]. pp. 19-20.

4 Ohtani, Koshin. "Seikatsu no nakade ojodo ga kanjirareru en ga daiji [The importance in having opportunities to feel the Pure Land in daily life]. Daijo, October 2006, pp. 6-7.

5 Suzuki, Daisetz. Jodo-kei Shiso-ron [Thoughts of Jodo Traditions]. p. 221.

6 Ibid., p. 223.

7 Uyeda, Yoshifumi. ed. The *True Teaching, Practice and Realization of the Pure Land Way*, Vol. III. p. 395.

8 Uyeda, Yoshifumi. ed. Notes on 'Essentials of Faith Alone.' p. 42.

9 Buddhist Churches of America 2009 Calendar. May 2009.

10 Hayashima, Kyosho. Ojojodo no gendaiteki kaimei [Contemporary Understanding of the Pure Land of Utmost Bliss]. p. 3.

11 Teramoto, Etatsu. Ichigu o terasu-mono [A Person Who Shed Light on a Small Corner]. pp. 13-14.

13 Uyeda, Yoshifumi. ed. Notes on the Inscriptions of the Sacred Name. p. 46.

[13] Taisho Shinshu Daizokyo (Taisho Edition Tri-Pitaka). Vol. 26, p. 232.

[14] Keenan, John P. tr. *The Summary of the Great Vehicle*. p. 105.

[15] Ibid., p. 105.

[16] Ibid., p. 114.

[17] Ibid.

[18] Nagao, Gadjin. Shodaijyo-ron–Wayaku to Chuge [The Mahayasamgraha–Its Japanese translation and commentary]. p. 415.

Jodo Shinshu Buddhism as a Global Religion in the 21st Century

In the past, the teachings of Jodo Shinshu Buddhism were sometimes considered pessimistic and difficult to propagate in the United States, due to their unique Japanese characteristics. However, Shin Buddhism has finally become a global religion, spreading all over the world. It teaches about Amida Buddha, who has Infinite Life (*Amitayus*) and Infinite Light (*Amitabha*). And since Infinite Life means "always" and Infinite Light means "everywhere," Jodo Shinshu Buddhism is a religion for all people in any place and at any time. Jodo Shinshu Buddhism, the teaching of Amida Buddha, is certainly a global religion.

Rev. Itsuzo Kyogoku became a minister of the Buddhist Churches of America in 1919 and propagated Jodo Shinshu Buddhism for the next 34 years in the United States. He died in 1953. But in the following year, *Bright Buddhism* (*Akarui Bukkyo*), a collection of his writings, was published. In the book's forward, Dr. Daisetz T. Suzuki wrote in praise of Rev. Kyogoku's dedication to the Buddhist movement and its propagation to the east. Dr. Suzuki also described the importance of the contributions of Mahayana Buddhism to the world civilization.

On the role of Mahayana Buddhism in world civilization, Dr. Suzuki quoted the first Columbia University Bicentennial Lecture delivered by the world-renowned 20th-century historian, Professor Arnold Toynbee, in New York. A synopsis of Dr. Toynbee's lecture was published in The *New York Times* on January 4, 1954. According to Dr. Toynbee, a great phenomenon of world civilization during the 20th-century is the rising power of Christianity in the West and of Mahayana Buddhism in the East, predicting that the future of world civilization would depend on these two religions, Christianity and Buddhism.

Dr. Suzuki continued, saying "The world cannot be saved by historical Christianity. It has to be a religion like Mahayana Buddhism, which is based on absolute freedom that is not bound by history, legends, and prophets. Otherwise, the liberation of the world is not possible."

Dr. Suzuki emphasized the importance of the global responsibility of Mahayana Buddhism. In order to establish real peace of the world, Mahayana Buddhism has to contribute much, that is to say, to make the world like the Pure Land. Then, during his Shinshu lecture at the New York Buddhist Church in the spring of 1958, Dr. Suzuki praised Jodo Shinshu Buddhism for being the culmination of Pure Land Buddhism. He stated that, in Jodo Shinshu Buddhism, we find a major contribution that the Japanese can make to the outside world and to all other Buddhist Schools.

Jennifer James, a *Seattle Times* columnist, quoted Dr. Albert Einstein in the March 12, 2000 issue, saying, "The religion of the future will be a cosmic religion. It should transcend personal God and avoid dogma and theology. Covering both the natural and the spiritual, it should be based on a religious sense arising from the experience of all things natural and spiritual as a meaningful unity... If there is any religion that could cope with modern scientific needs, it would be Buddhism."

As Dr. Toynbee, Dr. Suzuki, and Dr. Einstein indicate, I believe that Jodo Shinshu Buddhism as a global religion will be able to contribute to world civilization in the 21st century.

Bibliography

Fujiwara, Ryosetsu. The Way to Nirvana. Tokyo: The Kyoiku Shincho Sha, 1974.

Inagaki, Hisao, The Way of Nembutsu-Faith. Kyoto: Horai Association, 1996.

Jodo Shinshu Seiten: Chushakuban [Jodo Shinshu Scriptures: An Annotated Edition]. Kyoto:Hongwanji Shuppan-bu, 1988.

Kajiyama, Yuichi. Bosatsu to Iukoto [The Meaning of Bodhisattva]. Kyoto: Jinmon Shoin, 1984.

Matsubayashi, Hoshu Y., The *Sukhavativyuha Sutra*. Union City: Samgha Press, 1985.

Suzuki, Daisetz T., Shin Buddhism. New York: Harper & Row, Publishers, 1970.

The *Tanni-sho* [*Notes Lamenting Differences*]. Kyoto: Ryukoku University, 1962.

Uyeda, Yoshifumi, gen. ed. Hymns of the Dharma Ages: A Translation of Shinran's Shozomatsu Wasan Kyoto: Hongwanji International Center, 1993.

—. Hymns of the Pure Land: A Translation of Shinran's Jodo Wasan. Kyoto: Hongwanji International Center, 1991.

—. Hymns of Pure Land Masters: A Translation of Shinran's Koso Wasan. Kyoto: Hongwanji International Center,1992.

—. Notes on 'Essentials of Faith Alone': A Translationof Shinran's Yuishinsho-mon'i. Kyoto: Hongwanji International Center, 1979.

—. Notes on the Inscriptions on Sacred Scrolls: A Translation of Shinran's Songo Shinzo Meimon. Kyoto: Hongwanji International Center, 1981.

—. *The True Teaching, Practice and Realization of the Pure Land Way*: A Translation of Shinran's *Kyogyoshinsho*. 4 vols. Kyoto: Hongwanji International Center, 1983-1990.

Biography

- Born in Olaa, Hawaii, on December 30, 1935, as the oldest son of the late Rev. and Mrs. Shushin Matsubayashi. Due to my mother's poor health, I was sent back to my father's temple in Shimane Prefecture in Japan to be raised.
- Joined the United States Army in 1956 and was honorably discharged in 1958.
- Received a Bachelor of Arts degree in Buddhism from Ryukoku University in March 1962.
- Received a Master of Arts degree in Buddhist Studies from Kyoto University in March 1967.
- Awarded a Doctor of Education degree in Multicultural Education and Bilingual Education from the University of San Francisco in May 1984.
- Received the academic rank of Hokyo in the Jodo Shinshu Hongwanji-ha in November 1986.
- Became a minister of the Honpa Hongwanji Mission of Hawaii in September 1959, serving at the Hawaii Betsuin, the Kona Hongwanji Mission, and the Ewa Hongwanji Mission.
- In October of 1972, was transferred to the Buddhist Churches of America, serving at the Sacramento Betsuin, the Berkeley Buddhist Church, and the Southern Alameda County Buddhist Church.
- Served as Chairman of the BCA Ministers Association from 1988 to 1989.
- In addition to serving as a minister of the BCA, also taught Buddhism at the Institute of Buddhist Studies in Berkeley, California, from 1972 to 1982, and taught Asian Religious Literature at California State University in Sacramento from 1974 to 1978.

- Appointed as the Bishop of the Buddhist Churches of Canada.
- Served as resident minister of the White River Buddhist Temple.
- Served as resident minister of the Buddhist Temple of Salinas and the Monterey Peninsula Buddhist Temple from October 2000 to January 20, 2006.
- In January 2006, became Rimban (Head Minister) of the Seattle Betsuin Buddhist Church, and retired from there and the Buddhist Churches of America on July 31, 2010, becoming a Minister Emeritus.
- Served as full-time Retired Kaikyoshi Resident Minister of the New York Buddhist Church from October 1, 2010 to December 31, 2012.
- Family: Wife, Kyoko; Three Sons, Mike (Monica), Ken (Cathleen), and Hugh (Ivy); Six Grandchildren: Marcus, Matthias, Allison, Josie, Ethan, and Max.